A HEAVENLY VICTORIOUS LIFE:

RECEIVING CHRIST AS ALL FOR YOU, IN YOU, AND THROUGH YOU

A Heavenly Victorious Life:
Receiving Christ as all for you, in you, and through you

Published by: Der Überwinder-Verlag, Eschenweg 12a, 33813 Oerlinghausen, Germany

Book design 2013 by "THERISMOS" Sp. z o.o.
ul. Sztabowa 32, 50-984 Wrocław, Poland

For more information about the author and this message please visit this website: www.greg-violi.com/en

From this website you can contact and schedule speaking engagements with Greg Violi. You can also find videos and sermons from Greg Violi on www.erweckt.de with different translations.

CONTENT

Henry Law- Christ is all, the Gospel of the Pentateuch. "The Lord Jesus received is holiness begun; the Lord Jesus cherished is holiness advancing; the Lord Jesus counted upon as never absent would be holiness complete."

Major Ian Thomas- "There is something, which makes Christianity more than a religion, more than an ethic, and more than the idle dream of the sentimental idealist. It is this something, which makes it relevant to each one of us right now as a contemporary experience. It is the fact that Christ Himself is the very life content of the Christian faith. There are few things quite so boring as being religious, but there is nothing quite so exciting as being a Christian!"

This book has but one major purpose: that you, the reader, may encounter Christ on every page. Father God, may your all glorious Son be experienced as all and in all throughout this entire book. Holy Spirit, may you glorify Christ with revealing all that is now belonging to Him. Lord Jesus, may you glorify the Father, by taking absolute possession of the reader and revealing the Father's image within your body on earth.

This book is dedicated to the glory of the Father God, for He cannot and He must not give it to another.

CHAPTER 1

THE TWO ESSENTIAL VISIONS

"Where there is no vision, the people perish"

Proverbs 29:18a

If my Christianity does not work in my home; then it will not work anywhere else. Jesus said go home and tell them what great things God has done. The gift of the Holy Spirit will first make us witnesses of the resurrected Christ in Jerusalem. This refers to those closest to you. Beloved, for so many years we have claimed a gospel that had so much power that it could change the world. However, the sad truth has been that it has not even had enough power and life to change our own families. Christian families are so often hard and critical and the children rebellious. This can be either on the outside or the inside. Christians are in grave danger of horribly misrepresenting Christ in this world. There is practically no evidence that a Christian couple has any more love than a non- Christian couple. Statistics show that the divorce rate for a Christian couple is almost identical to a non-Christian couple. It has now been almost 35 years ago since Jesus started teaching me that my testimony about Him must begin at home. So, throughout this entire book, let it be known that the life of the risen Christ should first of all affect those closest to me. This must be kept in mind as you, the reader go through the pages of this entire book.

There are two essential visions that every person needs: the vision of the all pure, all holy, all mighty and all beautiful Lord Jesus Christ. The second vision that will always accompany this first vision is the vision of the impure, unholy, perverse and helpless self that is in the heart of each individual.

In the Bible, there are many examples of individuals that saw the Lord and each one that saw Him also had a revelation of themself.

ISAIAH

"In the year that King Uzziah died I saw also the Lord sitting upon a throne, high and lifted up and his train filled the temple. Above it stood the seraphim; each one had six wings; with twain he covered his face, and with twain he covered his feet, and with twain he did fly. And one cried unto another, and said, "Holy, holy, holy, is the Lord of hosts; the whole earth is full of his glory. And the posts of the door moved at the voice of him that cried, and the house was filled with smoke, then said I, Woe is me! For I am undone; because I am a man with unclean lips, and I dwell in the midst of a people of unclean lips; for mine eyes have seen the King, the Lord of Hosts."

Isaiah 6:1-5

Isaiah was a very holy and righteous prophet of the Lord. He could easily find the fault of others in the world and in the people of God. However, when his eyes saw the Lord in all of His majestic purity, he could only see his own filth and impurity. The prophet said he was undone and woe is me. These phrases are declaring that Isaiah saw he had no hope and he deserved to die. Isaiah's vision of God gave him a deep revelation of himself.

DANIEL

"And he said unto me, O Daniel, a man greatly beloved, understand the words that I speak unto thee, and stand upright: for unto thee am I now sent.

Daniel 10:11

Then I lifted up mine eyes, and looked, and behold a certain man clothed in linen, whose loins were girded with pure gold of Uphaz, His body also was like the beryl, and his face as the appearance of lightning, and his eyes as lamps of fire, and his arms and his feet like in colour to polished brass, and the voice of his words like the voice of a multitude." Therefore I was left alone, and saw this great vision, and there remained no strength in me; for my comeliness was turned in me into corruption, and I retained no strength.

Daniel 10:5-8

Daniel was a man on earth who was highly esteemed and loved in heaven. Although he was such a precious man of God, when he saw the pre-incarnate Christ, his splendor was turned into corruption and his strength left his body. Daniel's vision of Christ revealed to him that there is no similarity between the holy ones on earth and the Holy One in heaven!

JOB

> *"I have heard of thee by the hearing of the ears: but now mine eye seeth thee: Wherefore I abhor myself, and repent in dust and ashes."*
>
> Job 42: 5, 6

Job was so extremely righteous in the sight of God, that God said to the devil, "Have you considered my servant Job as you have been travelling throughout the whole earth?" (Job 1:7-9). God declared to Satan, *"There is no one like him in the earth, a perfect and an upright man, one that feareth God, and avoids evil"* (Job 1:8).

This servant of God said that he would never let go of his righteousness. Job mentions over 25 things that he did that exalted his goodness before men. (Job 29) Everything changed for Job when the Lord opened his spiritual eyes so that he could see God. As soon as Job could see the inner purity, power and extreme beauty of the Lord, all that he could do was to hate himself and repent deeply. (Job 42:6) He no longer saw any good in himself, because he saw that all goodness comes solely from the Holy One. Yet again, a vision of the Lord released a bright all-consuming vision of Job.

MOSES

> *"And he said, I beseech thee, show me thy glory."*
>
> Exodus 33:18

> *"And the Lord descended in the cloud, and stood with him there, and proclaimed the name of the Lord. And the Lord passed by before him, and proclaimed, the Lord, The Lord God, merciful and gracious, longsuffering, and abundant in goodness and truth, keeping mercy for thousands,*

> *forgiving iniquity and transgression and sin, and that will by no means clear the guilty; visiting the iniquity of the fathers upon the children, and upon the children's children, unto the third and to the fourth generation. And Moses made haste, and bowed his head toward the earth, and worshipped."*
>
> Exodus 34:5-8

> *"And the sight of the glory of the Lord was like devouring fire on the top of the mount in the eyes of the children of Israel."*
>
> Exodus 24:17

Moses met the God of fire and it was so terrible that Moses said, "I exceedingly fear and quake" (Hebrews 12:21). Even after the God of fire revealed himself several times to Moses, there was still a greater and deeper revelation of the glory of God that Moses needed. Moses needed a fuller, more complete unveiling of God´s glory. This unveiling would reveal something even greater than the fire of His holiness. It would reveal something that was hidden deep within the Father´s heart from before the creation of the world. This was the hidden beauty in the slain Lamb.

The Lord caused all of his goodness to pass in front of Moses; and he immediately bowed down and worshipped (Exodus 34: 8). In that moment Moses was beholding the arm of the Lord, the slain Lamb, this was the hidden mystery within the Father's bosom. This secret wisdom that has been buried within the Father's heart before angels or men were created. The hidden beauty, which is the greatest revelation of God's glorious self, is the eternal fact that the Judge is also the Redeemer.

Sin and rebellion have a price and someone must pay this price. God's moral government cannot tolerate evil and rebellion or it would collapse and anarchy would take over his universe. The One that has every legal right to judge and condemn is the very One that forgives and pardons. The One who could demand all subjects to serve *Him*, is the very One who is the greatest servant of all.

Moses the powerful and able leader, whose pride and anger killed the Egyptian. He thought that the Israelites would have known he was their deliverer. When he saw the Lord, he was transformed into the meekest man on earth. Once again a vision of the Lord unveils the reality of self.

JOHN

> *"And I turned to see the voice that spake with me. And being turned, I saw seven golden candlesticks; And in the midst of the seven candlesticks one like unto the Son of man, clothed with a garment down to the foot, and girt about the paps with a golden girdle. His head and his hairs were white like wool, as white as snow; and his eyes were as a flame of fire; And his feet like unto fine brass, as if they burned in a furnace; and his voice as the sound of many waters. And he had in his right hand seven stars; and out of his mouth went a sharp two-edged sword: and his countenance was as the sun shineth in his strength. And when I saw him, I fell at his feet as dead. And he laid his right hand upon me, saying unto me, Fear not, I am the first and the last: I am he that liveth, and was dead; and, behold, I am alive forevermore, Amen; and have the keys of hell and of death."*
>
> Revelation 1:12-18

This beloved Apostle of Jesus Christ, seeing the resurrected and glorified King in all of His majestic beauty fell at his feet as one dead. Once again, a vision of the all-glorious Lord causes an immediate reaction and a revelation of self.

Results of seeing the Lord:

- No confidence in one's own ability
- A hatred of even one thought that would exalt self
- A deep trust and expectation in the power and faithfulness of God
- A new understanding and expectation that God will do what I can not
- A deep cleansing of hidden areas of darkness
- A new found appreciation of the mercy of God
- A deep humbling of oneself
- A tremendous fear of God
- A greater revelation of the Supremacy of the great *I AM* within His universe

"Not by Might, nor by Power"

> *"Then he answered and spake unto me, saying, This is the word of the Lord unto Zerubbabel, saying, Not by might, nor by power, but by my spirit, saith the Lord of hosts."*
>
> Zechariah 4:6

Since every man´s way is right in his own eyes (Proverbs 16:2, 21:2), men will trust in their own ability to accomplish their goals in life. This self-reliance brings every person under a curse, because cursed is he who trusts in man (Jeremiah 17:5). The very first aspect of Satan´s heart of self-exaltation is to think I will ascend up (Isaiah 14:13). This inner strength to ascend up is wrongly assumed to be within one´s own power. Jesus, the perfect Son of man and Son of God declared He can do nothing out of Himself (John 5:19, 30).

When Adam ate from the forbidden tree he became independent of God and dependent on his acquired knowledge. The knowledge that comes from information is the fruit of eating from the tree of knowledge. This makes a person feel competent and self-sufficient. This knowledge puffs them up on the inside (1 Corinthians 8:1).

Men feel very capable of doing things when they *know* how and they feel extremely incapable if they *do not* know. The truth is that it is our birthright to *not know*. Our sufficiency should come from the guidance of the Holy Spirit and not from our own knowledge. Our own acquired knowledge will give us a false sense of self-sufficiency. Our knowledge will feed our pride, making us feel strong on the inside and ready for any battle. Many times, this feeling of self-sufficiency due to acquired knowledge blocks us from sensing our need of *Another*. This *other* is the Holy Spirit. If I don´t see myself as needy, I will be stubborn and independent of others and even God.

Let us look at a few examples of this self-sufficiency in the Bible

MOSES

Moses was trained in all the ways of Egypt and he was so strong that he could kill an Egyptian with ease. He was an eloquent and powerful speaker. With all of these qualities, he saw himself *capable* to deliver the people of God out of bondage. He was so confident in himself that he was surprised that the children of God did not recognize him as their deliverer (Acts 7:22-29).

Throughout this entire book, we will see that all the victory is the Lord´s. The battle belongs to the Lord. The glory belongs to the Lord. The source of our strength, righteousness, and life must be *only* the Lord. God *could not* and *would not* use Moses´ might or power.

PAUL

Paul was a totally committed, zealous servant of God. Unfortunately, the god he served for so many years was simply himself. He relied on his excellent learning (Philippians 3:5, 6), his wonderful godly teacher Gamaliel, and his own wisdom, to crush and dominate others (Acts 26:9-12).

One day Saul saw the glory of the risen, exalted Christ. His glory was so bright that it blinded Saul and suddenly he lost all of his might and power.

In one moment a strong capable person can suddenly lose everything (money, strength, ministry, family, peace, etc.). Now, Saul could not even walk without someone leading him in the right direction (Acts 9:8).

After Saul saw the Lord of Glory, his very nature was changed and therefore, his name (nature) became Paul. As revolutionary as this experience was, there still was a lot of his strength that needed to be exposed by God.

In II Corinthians 11:5 we find Paul declaring that he was not a whit behind the chief apostles. Many years later, we read in Ephesians 3:8, Paul stating that he was less than the least of all the saints. Finally, many more years later Paul makes an incredible statement, "This is a faithful saying, and worthy of all acceptation, that Christ Jesus came into the world to save sinners; of whom I am chief." (1 Timothy 1:15). Paul is declaring that this statement is worthy of all men accepting it that Jesus came to save sinners and that he himself was the chief of all sinners. Paul uses the present tense in referring to himself as chief of sinners. He did not use the past tense, but instead he used the present tense.

Paul´s transformation was so great that it totally changed the subject of his boasting. He started by boasting in his strength and power and he ended by only boasting in *his* weaknesses (II Corinthians 11:30, 12:5, 9, 10). What a complete change of mind. Paul understood that the Lord could not and would not use his strength or power.

PETER

Peter thought that the other disciples were capable of denying their Lord, but not him. He trusted in his power and might to not deny his Lord. (Luke 22:31-34). He had to be sifted like wheat by Satan. Jesus prayed for Peter that when he fell, his faith would stand. Then, after Peter recovered from his fall, he needed to strengthen his brethren. When God allows the evil one to sift you, it is because something is needed to be removed from your life. Many times, our self-confidence and self-sufficiency is the main thing that is needing to be removed. Peter had to discover that he was so weak that even a little girl could make him react in anger and fear. Once again, Peter had to learn the vital lesson that God cannot use our power or might.

The Bride in the Song of Songs

> *"Draw me, we will run after thee: the king hath brought me into his chambers....*
>
> Song of Solomon 1:4

> *"I am black, but comely, O ye daughters of Jerusalem, as the tents of Kedar, as the curtains of Solomon."*
>
> Song of Solomon 1:5

When the Groom takes the Bride into His secret chambers; then He allows her to see the secret dimensions of His love, His extreme holiness, His pure unselfishness and deep compassion.

When she beholds His depth of pure love, this brilliant light now exposes all hidden areas of darkness within her.

After entering into this Presence of pure light, she comes out with the astounding, but true and essential revelation that she is totally black. There is no good thing within her. She is as black as the nomadic tents in the desert, the filthy black tents of Kedar. With this essential revelation comes the other all-consuming vision of the glorious life of Christ within the bride. Now, she realizes that she is black, hopeless and corrupt in her flesh, but at the same time she is as lovely as the curtains of Solomon. There was nothing as lovely as these curtains, the exquisite beauty of the exalted Christ living in her as her very life. Knowing my total insufficiency is the door to experiencing the total sufficiency of my risen Lord.

By My Spirit, says the Lord of Hosts

> *"Then he answered and spake unto me, saying, This is the word of the Lord unto Zerubbabel, saying, Not by might, nor by power, but by my spirit, saith the Lord of hosts."*
>
> Zechariah 4:6

Apart from Jesus, we can do *nothing* (John 15:5), but through the Spirit of the risen Christ, we can do *all* things (Philippians 4:13). We can boast like Paul about all of our weaknesses so that the power of the risen Christ can rest on us constantly (II Corinthians 12:9, 10).

David had a main passion that drove him to win battle after battle. This burning passion was to reveal to the whole earth that there is a God that lives in His people. (I Samuel 17:46).

David begged God to not take His Holy Spirit away from him (Psalms 51). Hundreds of times David refers to the Lord as his God, Redeemer, High Tower, Shield, Refuge, and Rock. David knew that the Lord was his own faithful covenant keeping God. David had a trust in what his God could do through him. He understood that very victory must be the Lord fighting through him.

The Lord told Moses that "I am come down to deliver" (Exodus 3:8a). In other words, you cannot do this from your own source and ability, but I will do it through you. Even after the Lord told Moses that He had come to do the work, still Moses kept looking to himself. Moses needed to learn the same lesson that we all must learn. It is not by any power or might that we have, or think we have, but only by His Spirit. Almighty God will do by His Spirit whatever He is asking us to do.

When Jesus said to His disciples to be perfect as your Father in heaven is perfect (Matthew 5:48), he wasn´t lying, joking or deceiving. He meant every word that He spoke to them. This command to be perfect is referring to the perfection of love and it is to be obeyed and not rejected by any of God´s people! Now, the question should arise, how can we mortal human beings be perfect? The answer is: only by allowing the *Perfect Lover* to live in us.

The secret to all that Jesus asks of us is Himself. He is the missing factor in the equation. *"Faithful is he who calls you, who also will do it"* (I Thessalonians 5:24). Whatever the Lord Jesus calls us to do, He also promises to do in us and through us. This is the grace of God.

CHAPTER 2

WHAT IS THE CHRISTIAN LIFE?

The truth covered in this chapter can be stated to be the foundational stone of Christian doctrine. If this foundational stone is missing, then the entire building will eventually collapse. The Psalmist said “If the foundation be destroyed, what can the righteous do?” (Psalm 11:3). The apostle Paul said that there can be no other foundation laid, except the one that is already laid. (I Corinthians 3:11).

Therefore, what is the Christian life? Is it something that we are expected to do? Is it a kind of experience that we encounter in this world? Is it many different experiences that one goes through as he walks on this journey called life? Is it something that has differing levels depending on one's maturity and growth? Or is it something that is peculiar to people who attend religious gatherings on Sundays? The Christian life is none of the above. The Christian life is a quality of life or a kind of life. It is a kind of life that has its origin in another world and another dimension. The Christian life is not a something at all, but a *Someone.*

The Christian life is the very life of a person. The Christian life is a heavenly life with its source in a heavenly realm. The Christian life is the very life of Father God that has been deposited into His Son. The Father has given to His Son to have life in Himself. "For as the Father hath life in himself; so hath he given to the Son to have life in himself" (John 5:26). Jesus said that he could do nothing of himself. In the Gospel of John, Jesus makes reference to not doing anything out of His own ability at least 12 times. In this one gospel, Jesus was constantly making reference to his total dependence on His Father for everything. (John 5:19,30; 6:57; 7:17, 28; 8:28,42; 10:37-38; 12:44,45,49,50; 14:10; 17:8).

He even declared that if He spoke out from himself that this would be proof that he was seeking His own glory (John 7:17, 18a).

Jesus only did what he saw his Father doing. He only spoke what his Father spoke. He was a vessel for the life of His Father to live inside of Him. Jesus Christ so thoroughly manifested his Father that he said to His disciples if you see me, then you are beholding the Father. (John 14:9, 10; 17:6).

Father God had an eternal plan whereby His very life, power and image would be revealed within a body. There was an eternal covenant made between the Father, the Word and the Spirit. One of the phrases to describe this eternal covenant is "The Lamb slain from the foundation of the world." (Revelation 13:8, I Peter 1:17-20). This covenant had to be ratified in Blood and therefore when the Blood of Jesus Christ was shed, then He could make a triumphant cry, "It is finished." (John 19:30).

Through the new covenant in the blood of the eternal Lamb, God our Father has formed resurrection life and power into the body of His Son. Through Jesus, the Christ, the Father has accomplished all the desires of His heart.

There is now a new creation, a new humanity, one body, one sacrifice, and a new covenant. Everything that the heavenly Father desires can only be done in and through the life of his risen and exalted Son. By the Holy Spirit, Jesus lives in and through his body on earth. The eternal purpose of God was to have his uncreated eternal life expressed in and through a body on earth. This is not the same as created life. This is eternal, uncreated divine life or the very life of God himself being revealed and seen in creation. This is the image and life of God seen in and through mankind.

Now through redemption, man had been re-united with God to receive his very own life once again. The old creation that was controlled by the life of Adam through his natural soul can never please the heart of the Father. Men by nature receive a self-centered, self-exalting life of Adam. Men by redemption receive a self-less, God-exalting, God-centered life of Christ. The Christian life is the same exact life that was revealed in Jesus Christ while he walked on earth in his physical body about 2000 years ago. It is not something we do, but it is the very life of Someone right now at the right hand of the Father in heaven.

Please read prayerfully and slowly over the following scriptures:

> *"And this is the record, that God hath given to us eternal life, and this life is in his Son. He that hath the Son hath life; and he that hath not the Son of God hath not life."*
>
> 1 John 5:11-12

> *"In this was manifested the love of God toward us, because that God sent his only begotten Son into the world, that we might live through him."*
>
> 1 John 4:9

> *"I am crucified with Christ: nevertheless I live; yet not I, <u>but Christ liveth in me</u>: and the life which I now live in*

the flesh I live by the faith of the Son of God, who loved me, and gave himself for me."

Galatians 2:20

"For if, when we were enemies, we were reconciled to God by the death of his Son, much more, being reconciled, we shall be saved by his life."

Romans 5:10

"For if by one man's offence death reigned by one; much more they which receive abundance of grace and of the gift of righteousness shall reign in life by one, Jesus Christ."

Romans 5:17

"But thanks be to God, which giveth us the victory through our Lord Jesus Christ."

I Corinthians 15:57

"For to me to live is Christ."

Philippians 1:21

"For it is God which worketh in you both to will and to do of his good pleasure."

Philippians 2:13

"But my God shall supply all your needs according to his riches in glory by Christ Jesus."

Philippians 4:19

"For in him dwelleth all the fullness of the Godhead bodily."

Colossians 2:9

"For ye are dead, and your life is hid with Christ in God. When Christ, who is our life, shall appear, then shall ye also appear with him in glory."

Colossians 3:3-4

"Faithful is he that calleth you, who also will do it."

I Thessalonians 5:24

"Now unto him that is able to keep you from falling, and to present you faultless before the presence of his glory with exceeding joy."

Jude 1:24

"By the which will we are sanctified through the offering of the body of Jesus Christ one for all...For by one offering he hath perfected for ever them that are sanctified."

Hebrews 10:10, 14

"And what is the exceeding greatness of his power to us-ward who believe, according to the working of his mighty power, which he wrought in Christ, when he raised him from the dead, and set him at his own right hand in the heavenly places, far above all principality, and power, and might, and dominion, and every name that is named, not only in this world, but also in that which is to come: and hath put all things under his feet, and gave him to be the head over all things to the church, which is his body, the fullness of him that filleth all in all."

Ephesians 1:19-23

"And have put on the new man, which is renewed in knowledge after the image of him that created him:

> *where there is neither Greek nor Jew, circumcision nor uncircumcision, Barbarian, Scythian, bond nor free: but Christ is all, and in all."*
>
> Colossians 3:10-11

> *"Now the God of peace, that brought again from the dead of our Lord Jesus, that great shepherd of the sheep, through the blood of the everlasting covenant. Make you perfect in every good work to do his will, working in you that which is wellpleasing in his sight, through Jesus Christ; to whom be glory for ever and ever. Amen."*
>
> Hebrews 13:20-21

There is a growing pain deep within the soul of humanity. This pain is a yearning to see God the Father. One day Greek believers came to Philip and asked if they could see Jesus (John 12:21). This desire to behold the real Jesus in flesh and blood is the yearning that is within the hearts of people to touch the Father. Jesus is the exact representation of the Father and the express image of His person (Hebrews 1:3). Today, this world is starving to experience the Father's love within His Son.

Jesus gave the answer to the disciples as to how the world would see Him. His answer was the seed must be sown into the earth and then it would be multiplied into the world.

The incorruptible seed would grow and multiply within a body and this indestructible life of Christ would be dispensed throughout his body worldwide (John 12:24-26, Acts 12:24, Hebrews 7:16, Mark 4:3-20).

The world is wanting to see the real Jesus Christ, but so many within the church have opened their hearts to another Jesus, another spirit and another gospel (II Corinthians 11:4).

God the Father wants to see the Son in whom He is well pleased (Matthew 3:17), in the churches. However, so often He is watching another false Jesus appearing to be His glorious Son.

In order for someone to try to live the Christian life, that one must deny the very Christ; who is the life. There are not two kinds of resurrection life. There is only one kind of resurrection life. There are not two types of eternal life, there is only one type of life which is called eternal life. Divine or eternal or resurrection life is the very life of God and this is the real Jesus! Paul said to the Galatians, *"Are ye so foolish? having begun in the Spirit, are ye now made perfect by the flesh?"* (Galatians 3:3). The Christian life is the Spirit of God that brings the life of the ascended Christ into the body of a believer (I Corinthians 6:17, 19-21; I John 3:24, 4:13).Whenever a believer trusts in their own ability and relies on any aspect of their flesh to live the Christian life, they are denying their Lord the right to live inside of them.

The early church carried a message that was filled with wonder, glory, excitement and it was the fact that He is Risen. This message was accompanied by great power so that they could give witness to the fact that He is Risen indeed (Acts1:8, 2:31-33, 4:33). Jesus himself told His disciples that the whole world would know that they are truly His disciples by his very love being seen in them (John 13:34, 35; 17:26).

The question that each person must answer is: Am I going to deny self and receive the Risen Christ to live through me or am I going to deny Christ and allow self to live through me? (Luke 9:23) Who will I deny?

God the Father has accomplished a complete and thorough work in the person of His Son.

The Christian life is simply Christ Himself

When a person is reborn they are receiving Him, the Lord Jesus Christ and when they receive Him, they receive all that they need for life and for godliness (2 Peter 1:4, John 1:12).

He is their mercy, righteousness, sanctification, love, hope, peace, strength, redemption, wisdom and all that they will ever need now and forever. When an individual comes to Christ, he is joined to the Lord (I Corinthians 6:17). He is added to his body as a member of Christ. In the early church they were added to the Lord *"And believers were the more added to the Lord, multitudes both of men and women"* (Acts 5:14).Christ´s death becomes their death, Christ´s life becomes their life, Christ´s resurrection becomes their resurrection and Christ´s exaltation becomes their exaltation. The two become one and this is a great mystery (Ephesians 5:27-32).

Here are the words that the Apostle uses to summarize the entire meaning of church and Christianity: Christ is all! (Ephesians 1:23; Colossians 3:11) The entire summation of Christianity can be found in these three words: Christ is all!

CHAPTER 3

THE SATANIC SUBSTITUTE FOR THE REAL JESUS

Satan has provided a substitute to replace the risen, ascended Christ within the believer and his imitation is human goodness. Human goodness is a tremendous deception because it has an outward appearance of being so kind, pleasant, and righteous. It does not appear to be evil at all. It only has the outward appearance of being good. If human goodness gave the appearance of being evil, then it would lose its power to deceive others.

Scriptural References about Human Goodness

> *"The heart is deceitful above all things, and desperately wicked: who can know it?"*
>
> Jeremiah 17:9

> *"I said to the Lord, I have no good besides Thee"*
>
> Psalm 16:2 (NAS)

"Behold, I was shapen in iniquity; and in sin did my mother conceive me."

Psalm 51:5

But we are all as an unclean thing, and all our righteousness are as filthy rags; and we all do fade as a leaf; and our iniquities, like the wind, have taken us away"

Isaiah 64:6

"And a certain ruler asked him, saying, Good Master, what shall I do to inherit eternal life? And Jesus said unto him, Why callest thou me good? None is good, save one, that is, God. Thou knowest the commandments, Do not commit adultery, Do not kill, Do not steal, Do not bear false witness, Honour thy father and thy mother. And he said, All these have I kept from my youth up. Now when Jesus heard these things, he said unto him, Yet lackest thou one thing: sell all that thou hast, and distribute unto the poor, and thou shalt have treasure in heaven: and come, follow me. And when he heard this, he was very sorrowful: for he was very rich. And when Jesus saw that he was very sorrowful, he said, How hardly shall they that have riches enter into the kingdom of God! For it is easier for a camel to go through a needle's eye, than for a rich man to enter into the kingdom of God. And they that heard it said, Who then can be saved? And he said, The things which are impossible with men are possible with God."

Luke 18:18-27

"for that which is highly esteemed among men is abomination in the sight of God."

Luke 16:15b

Men are prone to think that God is pleased with the nature of man, but this is absolutely false. Probably the best description of human nature in the Bible is found in the next portion of Scripture.

> *"What then? Are we better than they? No, in no wise: for we have before proved both Jews and Gentiles, that they are all under sin; As it is written, There is none righteous, no not one: There is none that understandeth, there is none that seeketh after God. They are all gone out of the way, they are together become unprofitable; there is none that doeth good, no, not one. Their throat is an open sepulchre; with their tongues they have used deceit; the poison of asps is under their lips: Their feet are swift to shed blood: Destruction and misery are in their ways: and the way of peace have they not known: There is no fear of God before their eyes. Now we know that what things soever the law saith, it saith to them who are under the law: that every mouth may be stopped, and all the world may become guilty before God."*
>
> Romans 3:9-19

> *"For I know that in me (that is, in my flesh,) dwelleth no good thing: for to will is present with me; but how to perform that which is good I find not."*
>
> Romans 7:18

> *"That which is born of flesh is flesh; and that which is born of the Spirit is spirit."*
>
> John 3:6

These verses and many others are sufficient to reveal that God has no confidence in what man can do by his human nature. Man from birth is born with a sinful and self-exalting nature. Therefore, human goodness is a lie. There is nothing good in man. Adam was created in the image of God (Genesis 1:26) but, Adam had a son in his own image. (Genesis 5:3).

Adam's descendants inherited a twisted, demonic nature that is filled with selfish desires to be seen in a good way by others.

We saw in Romans Chapter 3 that both Jew and Gentile were absolutely similar in that not one of them sought God or did good.

All men refuse to do good and to acknowledge their evil nature.

> *"And you hath he quickened, who were dead in trespasses and sins; Wherein in time past ye walked according to the course of this world, according to the prince of the power of the air, the spirit that now worketh in the children of disobedience: Among whom also we all had our conversation in times past in the lusts of our flesh, fulfilling the desires of the flesh and of the mind; and were by nature the children of wrath, even as others."*
>
> Ephesians 2:1-3

The Beginning of Human Goodness (Part 1)

Human goodness was the result of Adam and Eve eating from the forbidden tree of the knowledge of good and evil. It was the deceitful fruit from this tree that instructed them to cover their sin with leaves. (Genesis 3:7)

God said to Adam, "Where are you?" (Genesis 3:9). Why did the Lord God say to Adam where are you? It was not because He was wondering where Adam had gone. Certainly not, for God knows everything and He knew exactly where Adam was located. God desired that Adam would uncover himself because if we uncover our sin and deception, then God will cover us with His mercy and glory (Psalm 32).

Human goodness provides us with a false covering that makes us feel good and safe. The truth is that as long as someone is covered by their own goodness (righteous deeds, outward acts, charm or religious performance) they are under the judgment of the Light.

God the Word covered Adam and Eve with His Light, but when they rejected His voice the glory of His light left them and they all of a sudden knew that they were uncovered or naked. (Genesis 3:7-10, John 1:1-9, Ephesians 5:13, I John 1:5)

Human goodness began in the Garden of Eden when our forefathers covered their sin and hid in the darkness. The Lord tried to bring Adam out of darkness into light by asking him, 'Where are you?'

The Judgment

> *"And this is the judgment, that light is come into the world, and men loved darkness rather than light, because their deeds were evil."*
>
> John 3:19

The judgment on the entire world is that men's hearts are evil and they hide in the darkness in order to cover their evil hearts.

The Pharisees would not go into the waters of baptism to let John baptize them because they rejected God's counsel against them. God's counsel was that they were no different on the inside, than any other sinner. Maybe, they appeared to be totally different on the outside, but on the inside they were identical to any other person.

> *"And all the people that heard him, and the publicans, justified God, being baptized with the baptism of John. But the Pharisees and lawyers rejected the counsel of God against themselves, being not baptized of him."*
>
> Luke 7:29-30

If the religiously righteous Pharisee would have walked into the water confessing his sins he would have been letting the whole world know that he was the same as those other sinners (publicans, prostitutes, drug addicts, etc.). The self-righteous Pharisee did not consider himself to be as evil as those other sinful people. But, the truth was that on the inside, his heart was extremely wicked, deceitful and full of all uncleanness, but it was all covered with human goodness! When John saw the Pharisees and Sadducees coming to his baptism to check things out, he rebuked them and called them a brood of snakes. In other words, in their blood line is the poison of the serpent. John was saying to them, the pride and arrogance is hidden inside of your heart and you must deal with this outward appearance of goodness and deeply repent on the inside before you can be baptized.

Human goodness will do all kinds of deeds outwardly as long as it can keep hidden in the darkness the truth of its inner heart attitudes.

> *"This is the judgment – that light is come into the world, but men loved darkness instead of the light because their deeds were evil. For everyone that does evil hateth the light neither comes to the light, lest his deeds are exposed."*
>
> John 3:19-20

Since all men want to appear as good in the eyes of others, they do not want the true Light to expose their evil. This is a hidden desire to receive *man's* approval instead of receiving *God's* approval.

> *"I receive not honour from men. But I know you, that ye have not the love of God in you. I am come in my Father's name, and ye receive me not: if another shall come in his own name, him ye will receive. How can ye believe, which receive honour one of another, and seek not the honour that cometh from God only?"*
>
> John 5:41-44

> *"Nevertheless among the chief rulers also many believed on him; but because of the Pharisees they did not confess him, lest they should be put out of the synagogue: For they loved the praise of men more than the praise of God."*
>
> John 12:42-43

The judgment is that the Light is come. Jesus has come as Savior, as Lord, as peace, as life, as victory, as our substitute, as our goodness, as our love and as the great "I Am". He is Jehovah, I AM. I am refers to the eternal sufficiency of the Son of God to be the supply of all the needs of his children. My God shall supply all your needs according to His glorious riches in Christ Jesus. (Philippians 4:19).

Jesus Christ is the Father's Gift to the world. He was ordained to be all that they need. He is "*I Am*". The Light is come and in the presence of the Light, we will discover that Jesus Christ is all purity, all goodness and all in all. We will also discover that we have no good thing and that deep within our hearts are divided motives, unclean thoughts and selfishness.

The Light will expose our tremendous failure, our great need, our selfishness and our emptiness. Hidden deep within human goodness is a deceitful heart full of uncleanness and lies. Many times hidden deeply under human goodness is a spirit of murder. When a person starts to really walk in the truth, they will love the Light and agree with the judgment of Light. This judgment declares that there is no good thing n man. Therefore, the Holy Spirit will have to create love, goodness and life in them and through them.

> *"But he that doeth truth cometh to the light that his deeds may be made manifest, that they are wrought in God."*
>
> John 3:21

The one loving the light has now become a vessel for the Light (truth) to shine through. Their earthly vessel now reveals the light and glory of God.

The Father has wrought a tremendous accomplishment in His Son. This accomplishment is a finished work and *all* that is necessary to bring pleasure to the very heart of Father God is contained within His glorious Son.

> *"Wherefore when he cometh into the world, he saith, Sacrifice and offering thou wouldest not, but a body hast thou prepared me...For by one offering he hath perfected for ever them that are sanctified."*
>
> Hebrews 10:5, 14

A Question of Source or Origin

Everything that has its origin in the nature of flesh is an abomination to God. God said to Abraham, *"Take now thy son, thine only son Isaac."* (Genesis 22:2a). God did not acknowledge the son conceived after the flesh, Ishmael. When we do works for God out of our flesh, God sees an unprofitable thing. *"The flesh profits nothing."* (John 6:63). These are dead works in the eyes of God (Hebrews 6:1). We are to repent from all of our unprofitable, dead works. The flesh cannot please God (Romans 8:8). It has no desire to please God, but only a hidden desire to be acknowledged and honored by men.

How can a person know what is the true motive of their heart? Our reactions when others despise, hate, or lie about us will reveal the true essence of what is inside of one′s heart. When human goodness is working in a person, they will feel hate and there will be a reaction of resentment or frustration on the inside. The inner attitude of hate will usually be covered with nice words. God says if a person has hatred inside they will cover it with nice words (Proverbs 26:24). One of the reasons human goodness is so wrong in God′s sight is because it takes the glory away from the Son of God and gives the glory to men. Human goodness loves to give recognition for the purpose of *receiving* honor and recognition from others in return. This attitude of my own goodness or self-righteousness will deceive me so greatly that I will actually offer to others my help, my love, my affection instead of just being a vessel for the real Jesus. Deep inside the deceived heart of human goodness is a hidden thought that what we can give people is as good as what the real Jesus could give them. The real living Christ will pour His love, His compassion, His faith and His life *through* me *into* others if I offer myself as a vessel. Human goodness will offer *itself* to meet the needs of humanity instead of bringing Christ to humanity′s needs. There is a real Christ who desires to give himself physically, financially, emotionally and spiritually to the world.

The world is crying, "we would see Jesus sir." (John 12:21). When a husband sees his wife, is he looking at Jesus in an earthen vessel? When a wife looks into her husband's eyes, is she looking into the eyes of Jesus? When a child looks at his mom or dad, are they beholding Jesus Christ? When the world looks at the church, the body of Christ (Ephesians 1:22, 23) are they seeing the real risen and ascended Christ Himself?

The Satanic substitute for the real Jesus (Part 2)

Satan has provided a substitute to replace the real Jesus Christ and it is human goodness. This is one of the best counterfeits that Satan could have created for several reasons:

- It looks like the real Jesus on the outside
- It does nice, good things that help others in life.
- It causes the one who has it to be totally unaware of its deceptive and wicked nature.
- It feeds and strengthens the main attitude of heart that God hates; which is pride (Proverbs 16:5).
- It is in total union with spiritual pride and therefore religious people who walk in pride will love it and wholeheartedly embrace the one who has it.
- It will accomplish Satan's goal to destroy the work of the kingdom of God because this attitude of goodness will cause the Father to resist us (James 4:6, I Peter 5:5).
- It keeps an individual in darkness, because true Light always opposes human goodness (Matthew 6:22-24).
- It creates and empowers another Jesus, another gospel and another spirit in the church (II Corinthians 11:4).

This human goodness hides the real, deep inner attitudes of anger and fear that are buried under the facade of goodness. These deep inner attitudes will only surface when someone seriously challenges the spirituality of the individual.

Maybe worst of all, is that the *real* Jesus is blocked from healing and transforming the broken hearts of multitudes. Since Jesus always reveals the Father, people will be blocked from coming into the Father's loving and precious presence.

The first encounter with the evil powers behind human goodness, was while I was ministering in a Christian gathering of a few hundred believers on a Sunday morning. This Sunday morning I sensed the fortress of demonic powers in the atmosphere, but I expected the Holy Spirit would start to dissolve and remove it. The demonic wall appeared impenetrable. The fortress of wickedness in that Christian assembly was so powerful that the wall would not move an inch! I was shocked and relieved when the service ended and all I could do was wonder, "What was that?"

The Lord clearly revealed to me at a later date, that the tremendous demonic fortress was the evil powers that were nicely hidden under the disguise of human goodness within the people of God. This was my first major encounter with the evil powers of human goodness.

What are some things that feed and strengthen human goodness in a person's life? What I am about to say might shock some readers, but please don't throw the book out and don't judge. The Holy Spirit never allowed my wife, Marie and I to tell our lovely girls that they were "good" little girls. Neither did we tell them that they were bad. We tried to speak the truth in love to them. Nowhere in the Bible will you find God telling His children that they are good by nature. Divine goodness should and will come through our lives by the Holy Spirit. Therefore, when a parent consistently tells their child that she is good this will feed human goodness within the child's heart.

It is also important to remember that *good people* are not in need of a Savior. But *sinners* have a tremendous need for a Savior. In Luke 7:36-50 we read about a Pharisee, a sinner and Jesus. The Pharisee manifested judgment on Jesus and the sinner. He was critical, uncaring, inconsiderate and hard -hearted. The sinner showed much brokenness, much sorrow for her sin, much love, thankfulness, much affection for Jesus and a deep desire to only consider the beautiful feet of the Savior. Jesus stated an eternal truth: *"To whom little is forgiven, they love little"* (Luke 7:47) and therefore he implied to whom much is forgiven they will love much. If I believe I am good, then I will only be conscious of my need of a little forgiveness and therefore I will only love a little.

Human goodness usually fills people with a deep sense of their own goodness and therefore they are usually not aware of their need for the mercy of God. This is why people with human goodness are usually hard hearted.

Things that contribute to hardness of heart:

- Teaching that ignores repentance.
- Services with no weeping and a negative attitude towards brokenness

Charles Spurgeon said when mister wet eyes leaves the church then you know the Holy Spirit has left. He was emphasizing the great need for weeping

- Fellowshipping with others who do not confess their sins.
- Encountering God's grace without ever sensing God's holiness
- Knowing only the love of God without any revelation of God as a consuming Fire (Hebrews 12:29)
- Having no revelation of God as Light (I John 1:5)

When the manifest Presence comes in to the service, He will

always expose the ugliness of human goodness. Therefore, if there is not a manifestation of the Presence then human goodness could thrive in a gathering.

We have seen the manifest presence of Christ melt hardened hearts thousands of times! Without a revelation of the Word human goodness will remain hidden in the heart of men. The Word is alive and a Judge of the thoughts and intentions of the heart (Hebrews 4:12, 13). If a Christian seldom ever reads the Word of God and just relies on his experiences or feelings, then he will have human goodness hidden in his heart. The main example of people deceived and filled with human goodness in the Bible are the Pharisees and Sadducees.

The Necessity of Rebuke that Demonstrates Pure Love

> *"As many as I love, I rebuke and chasten; be zealous therefore, and repent."*
>
> Revelation 3:19

Pride and selfishness is the main evil that corrupts human nature. Selfishness can have an outward appearance of being really bad or an outward appearance of being really good. *Good* self will try to do good religious things instead of *allowing* Christ do them in an earthen vessel. My sense of my own goodness will encourage me to draw from *myself* instead of drawing from the eternal well (John 4:14).

At the time of Jesus′ birth, the religious leaders were consumed with a deep sense of their own goodness. I never could understand why Jesus was so severe in His rebukes and chastening of the religious leaders of his day. Now I understand that these severe rebukes were truly the love of God for the

Pharisees and Sadducees. I can see now how this was their only hope. The Pharisees were in gross darkness, but they thought that they were in great light. What could a person convict a Pharisee of outwardly? He fasted twice a week, he always attended services at the synagogue, he prayed consistently, he sought the Lord, and he read the Scriptures. His outward behavior, like the Apostle Paul, was blameless concerning righteousness by the law (Philippians 3:6).

No human being would have been able to correct or rebuke a Pharisee about anything. He knew how to act and how to behave on the outside. He was totally convinced he was chosen by God and pleasing to God. His life was given for one main purpose; to serve and to please the true God of the universe. His pride and goodness had convinced him that his actions were justified by the law of God. He was highly esteemed in the eyes of others and in his own eyes as well. The Pharisee had convinced himself that the ends justified the means. In other words, if his actions were hard or severe, but the end result was to eradicate evil, then his evil attitudes served a *good* purpose in life and were acceptable to God.

These attitudes are the same as the Israelites that God rebuked in Isaiah 58.

> *Cry aloud, spare not. Lift up your voice like a trumpet and declare to My people their transgression and to the house of Jacob their sins! Yet they seek, inquire for, and require Me daily and delight[externally] to know My ways, as [if they were in reality] a nation that did righteousness and forsook not the ordinance of their God. They ask of Me righteous judgments, they delight to draw near to God [in visible ways]. Why have we fasted, they say, and You do not see it? Why have we afflicted ourselves, and You*

> *take no knowledge [of it]? Behold [O Israel], on the day of your fast [when you should be grieving for your sins], you find profit in your business, and [instead of stopping all work, as the law implies you and your workmen should do] you extort from your hired servants a full amount of labor. [The facts are that] you fast only for strife and debate and to smite with the fist of wickedness. Fasting as you do today will not cause your voice to be heard on high. Is such a fast as yours what I have chosen, a day for a man to humble himself with sorrow in his soul? [Is true fasting merely mechanical?] Is it only to bow down his head like a bulrush and to spread sackcloth and ashes under him [to indicate a condition of heart that he does not have]? Will you call this a fast and an acceptable day to the Lord?*
>
> Isaiah 58:1-5 Amplified Version

Through the centuries, the darkness had grown darker and darker in the hearts of the religious leaders. Now, when the Messiah came as the Light of the world, his very life and his words were the means whereby the Holy Spirit totally uncovered what was buried in the heart of the religious leaders. Two main ways to uncover the nature of sin hidden in the heart is the manifest presence of Christ and the pure Word of God. *"If I had not come and spoken to them, they had not had sin: but now they have no covering for their sin"* (John 15:22).

The presence of Jesus and the pure word spoken by Jesus totally uncovered the nature of sin or the attitude of pride that consumed the Pharisees' heart. What was covering the wickedness of sin that was hidden in the heart? Human goodness was the false covering that the religious leaders used to cover their sin.

Paul, the ex-Pharisee taught that every time we take the covenant meal, we were to partake with sincerity and truth.

"Therefore, let us keep the feast, not with old leaven, neither with the leaven of malice and wickedness; but with the unleavened bread of sincerity and truth" (1 Corinthians 5:8). Jesus said, all true worshippers must worship God in spirit and truth (John 4:24). The word that Paul used for sincerity literally meant "without wax". In Paul's day of commercial trading, if a seller had a small crack in a vase that he wanted to sell and he was not sincere, then he would put wax over the crack and cover it so that the buyer would not see it. However, if the vase was put under the light and there was no crack and no wax, then this seller was considered sincere. He had nothing to cover and nothing to hide.

David was another person in the Bible that had nothing to hide. He would even write a song for the choir to sing that described his sinful heart, like Psalm 51. David said, *"I will confess my iniquity and be sorry for my sin"* (Psalm 38:18).

Paul said, that in the presence of Christ, every hidden thing of darkness and every hidden counsel of the heart will manifest in the light (1 Corinthians 4:5). Transparency describes the heart of a true worshipper of God. A transparent person is covering nothing and therefore, they have nothing to hide. Since man's fall in the Garden of Eden, mankind has been hiding in darkness and blaming others for their sin. The Lord is saying to all people, but especially to religious people, "Where are you?", "Come out of darkness into the light", "Hide and cover nothing". Our wonderful Lord and Father will always cover our honest mistakes, but He will never cover our pride.

Many times we find the Holy Spirit uncovering the hidden pride of the religious heart. Jesus would heal someone or raise someone from the dead and afterwards the religious leaders would go outside and hold a meeting. In this religious meeting they would discuss how they might kill or destroy Jesus. The Holy Spirit tells us this many times in the gospels. No one would ever know how wicked the Pharisee's heart was unless the Spirit of God had one of the Gospel writers record it. The Word of God also says that Jesus would *answer them*. Now, since their physical lips were not asking any question, then what was Jesus answering? He was answering or responding to what their wicked heart was thinking. *"As a man thinks within his heart, so is he"* (Proverbs 23:7).

Human goodness may even try to be like Jesus on the outside, *even with the right intentions*. Sadly, it never can compare to the true love, compassion, mercy, holiness and kindness of Jesus Christ. Many times, this outward form of human goodness becomes a covering for hidden hatred. *"He that hates disguises it with his lips and lays up deceit within his heart"* (Proverbs 26:24).

Why will we cover our hatred? The answer lies in the fact that we do not want others to know the true condition of our heart. Human goodness will cause us to speak nicely and graciously to others, so that they will not know what is really in our heart. *"When he speaks graciously, do not believe him, for there are seven abominations in his heart"* (Proverbs 26:25). What are the seven abominations hidden in the heart of someone that covers his hatred with human goodness? A proud look, a lying tongue (deceit), hands that shed innocent blood (gossip), a heart that thinks evil, feet that are quick to run to evil (part of problem, instead of part of the solution), a false witness (people that mix truth with deceit) and he that sows discord and division into the hearts of brothers in the church (Proverbs 6:16-19). All of these evil attitudes are buried under the disguise of human goodness.

Jesus used such phrases as:

1. Whitewashed tombstones, (graves covered over with paint), beautiful on the outside, but dead and stinking on the inside (Matthew 23:26-28)

2. Hypocrites (Matthew 23; Luke 6)
3. Fools and blind guides (Matthew 23:19)
4. Pretense in your prayers (not real like sinners) (Matthew 23:14)
5. You will travel hundreds of miles just to make one disciple, then you make him twice the son of hell that you are. (Matthew 23:15)
6. You belong to your father; the devil (John 8:7).
7. You do the very lusts of your father; the devil (John 8)
8. You murder and lie, just like your father the devil (John 8)

These are just some of the many things that our Lord said to the religious leaders who covered their sinful heart with human goodness. After all these years; I now understand the importance of Jesus speaking strong rebukes to the religious leaders. It was not hate; it was extreme love and concern for their welfare (Revelation 3:19).

No other human on earth would have spoken such truth to them. The ungodly fear of men would prevent most individuals from speaking truth of this sort. They were covered by human goodness and this false covering caused them to believe a lie and not see the attitudes of their heart, which is the only thing that God looks at in us. (I Samuel 16:7, Jeremiah 17:9-10, Matthew 15:13-20, Mark 7:20-23, Revelation 2:23)

Am I Covered With My Own Goodness or the Glory of God in Christ Jesus?

The mercy seat is always beckoning sinners to draw near to it. The mercy of God is the place where His glory dwells because it comes to man through the blood of his Son. Self-righteous people find their glory in themselves but, sinners find their glory in the Lamb of God. When I confess my sins, the strange thing is that the mercy and glory of God will cover my shame. His glory is his mercy and compassion. Whenever a person walks in truth, and have no desire to reveal who they are, but only to show the world Jesus; then the glory of Jesus will cover me and come through my life. To walk in truth is to walk in light and to walk in the light is to be continuously cleansed by His blood (I John 1:7, 9).

John said that if a believer says he has no sin (nature), then he is deceived and the truth is not in him (I John 1:8). On the other hand, someone that does not want to hide their pride, but every time it manifests, they take the blame and confess their sin (I John 1:9), then these people are clean, filled with light, glory and truth and have great peace! Those who do not see their sin and do not take the blame are probably covered with human goodness and are likely trying to shine for Jesus instead of letting Him shine through them!

If *I* am trying to shine *for* Jesus, then this is light that is coming from me. Instead, if I am a vessel for Jesus then He will shine his pure light through me.

Jesus is the embodiment of pure love. The Word of God says such things as love is patient. How often is love patient? Always! Love is kind. How often is love kind? Always! Love never seeks its own. How often does God's pure love seek it's own? Never! If it is the real Jesus living in a believer, than He will always love with pure love through them. This is why the great Apostle Paul could say that he was the chief (present tense) of all sinners and that Christ lives in him (I Timothy 1:15, Galatians 2:20).

Is human goodness shining through me, or is it the risen, exalted, glorious Christ? The Christian life is a Person. The Christian life is the life of the resurrected Christ through His Spirit taking up residence in his body. It is Christ and it is not *something* to be attained, it is *someone* to be received. John said, "To as many as received Him, to them gave He the right to become the sons of God" (John 1:12).

The Christian life is a glorious reality that comes through a radiant, living Christ and He Himself is the supplier of all needs.

No Honey, No Leaven, but Lots of Salt.

> *"No meat offering, which ye shall bring unto the Lord, shall be made with leaven: for ye shall burn no leaven, nor honey, in any offering of the Lord made by fire."*
> *"And every oblation of thy meat offering shalt thou season with salt; neither shalt thou suffer the salt of the covenant of thy God to be lacking from thy meat offering: with all thine offerings thou shalt offer salt."*
>
> Leviticus 2:11, 13

The offerings had to be salted and there could be no leaven or honey in the offerings. What is the spiritual meaning behind salt? First of all, King Artaxerxes made a decree throughout all the land that everything needed in order to rebuild the house of God in Jerusalem be given to Ezra so that he may rebuild true worship in God's temple.

> *"And I, even I Artaxerxes the king, do make a decree to all the treasurers which are beyond the river, that whatsoever Ezra the priest, the scribe of the law of God of heaven, shall require of you, it be done speedily, Unto an hundred talents of silver, and to an hundred measures of wheat. And to an hundred baths of wine, and to an hundred baths of oil, and salt without prescribing how much."*
>
> Ezra 7:21-22

Unlimited salt was prescribed by Ezra, the priest and King Artaxerxes responded by stating that there should be salt without limit for the rebuilding of the house of God. We have an unlimited Christ as our possession.

The writer of Hebrews says that we, the people of God, are the house of God (Hebrews 3:6). Today there is a tremendous need to rebuild the house of God in the land. The church must come to a place of restoration and this will only come as the sacrifice is seasoned with much salt. There can be no honey or leaven, but there must be much salt. The spiritual meaning behind leaven is hypocrisy. The spiritual meaning of honey is human goodness and the spiritual meaning behind salt is the life of the risen Christ.

Jesus said that his body of believers were the salt of the earth (Matthew 5:13). The very fragrance of the risen Christ is inside of a believer and it is this fragrance that makes others thirsty and hungry for God. When the Father sees a Christian, he smells the fragrance of his Son in them. All throughout the Old Testament the smell of the burnt offerings were a sweet smelling aroma in the nostrils of God. Why? Because every time that Father God smelled the burnt offering, he was smelling and seeing His Son´s sacrificial offering of Himself on the altar. A Christian is a part of the body of Christ and so he partakes of the body of Jesus crucified, risen and exalted at the right hand of God.

> *"Now thanks be unto God, which always causeth us to triumph in Christ, and maketh manifest the savour of his knowledge by us in every place. For we are unto God a sweet savour (fragrance) of Christ, in them that are saved, and in them that perish: To the one we are the savour of death unto death; and to the other the savour of life unto life."*
>
> II Corinthians 2:14-16

The Father smells the very fragrance of his Son in the believer. They have been joined to Christ in his death and in his resurrection. While a believer is allowing the risen Christ to live in and through them; then He is releasing his savour and they become the salt of the earth. The salt represents the very life of the risen Christ.

As the beautiful Jesus shines through us; the Father smells the fragrance of Christ and the world is beholding Christ. To some, this fragrance of Jesus is a fragrance of life. When they smell Jesus and see Jesus shining in a believer´s body, they are smelling life. They are also yearning for His life to shine through them. When they see this life in another; he reminds them of the beautiful Christ. To others who love themselves and do not want to die, when they smell this risen Christ in a believer, it is a constant reminder that they themselves must die, so that Christ can shine through them. Since they have no desire to die, all they can smell is death. They cannot see that when they die, Christ lives in them. To some this fragrance reminds them of their need to die, and to others this fragrance reminds them of Christ and his beautiful life. Isaiah said that Jesus is beautiful to some, but he has no beauty to others (Isaiah 33:17, 53:2).

Unless someone forsakes all that he has in himself and no longer trusts in what he can do, he cannot be Jesus' disciple. I can put no confidence in anything coming out of my own flesh (Luke 14:33, 34; Philippians 3:3). The Father wants to smell the beautiful fragrance of His glorified Son in the church today. The world wants to see the beautiful Christ risen and alive in His body on earth.

Leaven is forbidden

> *"In the mean time, when there were gathered together an innumerable multitude of people, insomuch that they trod one upon another, he began to say unto his disciples first of all, Beware ye of the leaven of the Pharisees, which is hypocrisy."*
>
> Luke 12:1

The word that Jesus used for hypocrisy means a play actor. Someone who is playing the part or someone that is trying to make others think they are someone else. Brothers and sisters, when we are trying to live like Jesus; this is the leaven of the Pharisees! If my trust and dependence is on myself, my goodness, my religiosity, my talents, and not totally dependent on Christ living in me, then I am living just like the Pharisees. God does not want the leaven of hypocrisy or play acting in any offering as a substitute for his Son. Instead, He desires to see the real Jesus.

Honey has sweetness, doesn't it? Human goodness can have such a gentle sweetness. It has been said beware of too much sugar, for it will poison your system. Sugar is poison to your body and too much sugar can destroy the body. Jesus desires no human goodness in the offering; just the real life of Christ Himself.

> *"The words of his mouth were smoother than butter, but war was in his heart: his words were softer than oil, yet were they drawn swords."*
>
> Psalm 55:21

The Bible tells us that there was once a place where the land looked beautiful on the outside. It was pleasant to behold, but year after year it was just about to bear fruit and then it would miscarry. The water looked like it was full of life, but it was deceptive, for it too was dead. The water and land looked wonderful on the outside, but the truth is that they had no life.

> *"And the men of the city said unto Elisha, Behold, I pray thee, the situation of this city is pleasant, as my lord seeth: but the water is naught, and the ground barren (given to miscarriage). And he said, Bring me a new cruse, and put salt therein. And they brought it to him. And he went forth unto the spring of the waters, and cast the salt in there, and said, Thus saith the Lord, I have healed these waters; there shall not be from thence any more death or barren land."*
>
> II Kings 2:19-21

The Word of God and the salt have the secret to destroying the power of death and barrenness.

> *"So Moses brought Israel from the Red sea, and they went out into the wilderness of Shur; and they went three days in the wilderness, and found no water. And when they came to Marah, they could not drink of the waters of Marah, for they were bitter: therefore the name of it was called Marah. And the people murmured against Moses, saying, What shall we drink? And he cried unto the Lord; and the Lord shewed him a tree, which when he had cast into the waters, the waters were made sweet."*
>
> Exodus 15: 22-25

God has provided the tree (cross) for the bitterness of life. When someone comes to the cross and receives the mercy and love of Jesus Christ, they will have their bitterness healed. Just to understand how much God loves us in our sin and rebellion will break our hearts. Yes, the cross is the answer for all bitterness and bitter waters of life. On the other hand, the Salt is the answer for the barren land. In order to bear fruit; we need the risen and exalted Christ to live His life in and through us. Hosea 14:8 says, *"From me is thy fruit found."*

Jesus said that He was the Rock in the wilderness and he who is thirsty can come to Him and drink. This implies faith. In order for me to drink from the spiritual Rock, I must believe that He will release the waters. He that is drinking out of his innermost being shall flow rivers of living water (John 7:37-39). Only the real and wonderful Jesus can satisfy the thirst of a dying world. I must deny myself, and then I will discover the living Christ reigning and manifesting through my body (II Corinthians 4:10-12). My dear brother and sister, does your land have a pleasant appearance, but there is *no* fruit? Do you look good on the outside, but dying and barren on the inside? Are you doing all the right things, but there is no tangible fruit? Are your children changed? Is your family being transformed? Is your life affecting the lives of others? Are you seeing fruit being born in others? Do you need salt? Jesus will enrich your life if you will let him live his life through you.

CHAPTER 4

AM I LIVING BY MY WILL OR AM I LIVING BY HIS LIFE?

The famous Hindu leader Mahatma Gandhi rejected Christianity because he felt that Christians did not live what they taught. Once, E. Stanley Jones, the Christian missionary to India for over 50 years asked Ghandi, *"How can we naturalize Christianity in India, not a foreign thing, identified with a foreign government and a foreign people, but a part of the national life of India and contributing its power to India's uplift? Gandhi responded with great clarity and directness. "First, I would suggest that all of you Christians, missionaries and all, must begin to live more like Jesus Christ. Second, practice your religion without adulterating it or toning it down. Third, emphasize love and make it your working force, for love is central in Christianity."* [1]

These were three main things that Ghandi said must happen for Christianity to become an effective force in India. Although, these points are very important, I would have to add that my trying to live like Jesus will not change others. I must take all

[1] "Gandhi - Portrayal of a Friend" by E. Stanley Jones

the blame for not revealing Jesus to others, but then I must trust Jesus Himself to live His own risen and pure life through me. It is the pure life of Jesus Christ that will change others and not my imitation of Jesus.

The Apostle Paul said, *"...that to will is present with me; but how to perform that which is good, I find not"* (Romans 7:18). Paul chose to do what was right in God's eyes, although he made the right choice, he did not have the power to perform it in himself. A person can live by their willpower and consistently make the right choices, but this is not the same as living by His very life.

If I am as a Christian making the right choices, on the outside, then I will feel a certain satisfaction in myself. My mind will feel good about my Christianity, but my heart will feel a certain hardness and emptiness. I might have much confusion regarding my spiritual life because I am doing all that I know to do to please God, but still it does not seem to be working. I need to ask myself one major question, where am I focusing? Where is my focus? Is it on me and what I need to do, or is it on Him and all that He has done and is doing by his Holy Spirit? This is a very important question. There is a spiritual law that we set in motion every time our focus is on our self. *"I find then a law, that, when I would do good, evil is present with me"* (Romans 7:21). Paul is saying that every time he puts his focus on himself to do good, he activates the spiritual law of sin within his earthy members (Romans 7:25b). In our flesh is no good thing, therefore, whenever we are depending on our own ability to do good, it can only be human goodness. It will always have a hidden desire to be seen of men and honored by people.

The main characteristic of God's nature of love is to be always seeking the good of others and not itself (I Corinthians 13:5).

Our flesh will always seek something for itself, even if it is just a little "thank you" from someone. However, the Lord said to give expecting nothing in return. Jesus said to love your enemies, do good to those who spitefully use you, give expecting nothing back. Be perfect just as your Father in heaven is perfect. Be holy just as God is holy. We are commanded to do all of these things and many more. How is this possible? With man this is impossible; but with God all things are possible!

There is a hidden factor in the Christian life; it is the very ascended, risen and living Christ himself that is simply looking for a temple to live inside of. We must make the right choices, but after I choose I must trust the Holy Spirit to do it inside of me. This is how Jesus Christ lived His entire life on earth. He said that, "I can do nothing of myself" (John 5:19, 30). I only say what I hear the Father saying. I only do what I see the Father doing. I speak not out of myself, but I always speak out of the Father Himself, and this is through the Spirit of God. *"How much more shall the blood of Christ, who through the eternal Spirit offered himself without spot to God, purge your conscience from dead works to serve the living God?"* (Hebrews 9:14). Jesus offered himself to the Father through the eternal Spirit. We must make the right choices, but to live by our will alone will make us proud, hard, unfeeling Christians.

Grace is all-inclusive. The more fully one comprehends the true grace of God, the more clearly will they see that everything good in their life is purely a result of God´s grace on their behalf. The fact that we have breath is the grace of God. The ability to write and to read and to comprehend is the grace of God. Our power to make right choices is God working in me "to will" (Philippians 2:13). It is God´s grace that instructs us to live godly, soberly and righteously in this present evil world (Titus 2:11, 12).

God's marvelous grace is so undeserved and yet it is so abundant. While Jesus hung on the cross in the greatest possible agony, he was begging forgiveness in His behalf for all men. Due to Christ's sacrifice on the cross, the Father can now lavish his abundant grace on all that will simply receive it.

One of the best ways to learn grace is to find how much you need it because of your personal failures. It is when we have failed, that the Father wants to extend tremendous mercy and grace. I did not learn grace in my Bible school in America; I learned grace from my loving heavenly Father in the midst of my failures. Paul said that he was what he was only through the grace of God in his life (1 Corinthians 15:10).

When a person is looking to *their* will, and make the right decision, they are satisfied and can even become complacent. On the other hand, when a person understands that everything that they do is dependent on the grace of God, then they are constantly depending and trusting on God's grace in them. God will never disappoint the needy soul. He will be their supply in all that they need. The church in Laodicea came to the point where they *thought* they had need of nothing (Revelation 3:14:20). The religious leader of Jesus' day had made so many good choices they stopped guarding their hearts and they allowed their hearts to grow very cold.

Even success in the area of choices can cause a person to exalt themselves in what they have accomplished; instead of seeing our ever-present, all sufficient Savior!

My will can be the very strength of my life. If I am only seeing the importance of making right choices and if I am depending on my choices to affect others, I could totally miss my purpose in life. My calling and purpose in this life is to be a dwelling place for the very presence of the living God. I am to release His life to others. Others need His life. Our children need to touch the very life of God in us. Our spouses need to experience God's life through us. Our neighbors and our brothers and sisters in Christ are hungering and needing to be changed by the life of God that is coming through us into them. This is what Paul was referring to when he said, *"Death works in us, but life in you"* (2 Corinthians 4:12). As we accept our sentence of death (2 Corinthians 1:9, Galatians 2:20; Romans 6:11), then the life of the risen Christ will manifest through our physical bodies.

Dear brothers and sisters in Christ, there is a tremendous supply of Christ Jesus' Spirit of life in each one of us (Philippians 1:19, Romans 8:2). It is only our pre-occupation with our self and our fleshly desires (all those things that satisfy us both bad and good) that stops us from expecting the real Jesus to come through us daily! He is risen! He is alive in His church today. We are His temple so that He can live inside of us. *"But as many as received Him, to them gave he the power to become the sons of God, even to them that believe on his name; which were born, not of blood, nor of the will of the flesh, nor of the will of man, but of God"* (John 1:12,13).

Dear brothers and sisters, do we see His very life driving, enabling, and transforming us and others through us? Instead are we seeing all that we have done, all that we must do, and all that we can do for God? Whatever I am beholding becomes what governs my heart. If I am beholding the glory of the risen and exalted Lord in myself and others, then I am being changed into the very same image from glory to glory (2 Corinthians 3:18). If we are beholding all that we must do, then we will start to be consumed by a deep sense of self (either self-importance or self-anger) and we will look at all the things that others should be doing. Our attitude will lack the joy of the Lord.

The Psalmist tells us in Psalm 34:5, *"they looked to him and were radiant."* If we are looking to Him, His total sufficiency for us, in us, and through us, we will radiate his light and glory. Am I living by the power of my will or by the power of His life?

CHAPTER 5

A HEAVENLY LIFE AND A HEAVENLY SOURCE

There are two basic ways in which Christians choose to live their lives. A Christian can live in the heavenly realm, abiding in Christ, or by living out of the self-life in the earthly realm. The first way will bring the resources of heaven and the second way will bring the resources of earth. The first way will bear much fruit and glorify Christ. The second way will bear no fruit and bring much confusion. The first way is totally dependent on the Holy Spirit and the second way is dependent on the flesh. The first way releases a spiritual ministry and the second way releases a soulish ministry. Let us look closer at this subject.

The Heavenly Realm

The body of Christ has been raised with its head to heavenly places. *"And hath raised us up together in heavenly places in Christ Jesus."*

Ephesians 2:6

> *"If ye then be risen with Christ, seek those things which are above, where Christ sitteth on the right hand of God. Set your affection on things above, not on the things on the earth. For ye are dead, and your life is hid with Christ in God."*
>
> Colossians 3:1-3

> *"What is the exceeding greatness of his power toward us who believe, according to the working of his mighty power, Which he wrought in Christ, when he raised him from the dead, and set him at his own right hand in the heavenly places, Far above all principality, and power, and might, and dominion, and every name that is named, not only in this world, but also in that which is to come: And hath put all things under his feet, and gave him to be the head over all things to the church, Which is his body, the fullness of him that filleth all in all."*
>
> Ephesians 1:19-23

The body is seated with their Lord and their head in heavenly places. Joined in this union with the exalted Christ, they are to put on his very image.

> *"The first man is of the earth, earthy; the second man is the Lord from heaven. As is the earthy, such are they also that are earthy: and as is the heavenly, such are they also that are heavenly. And as we have borne the image of the earthy, we shall also bear the image of the heavenly."*
>
> II Corinthians 15:47-49

Paul is admonishing the church of Corinth that it is time to put on their ascended Lord. Just as they have manifested the nature of the first man, Adam. Now, it is time to manifest the very nature of the Second Adam. John said, *"...as He is so are we in this present world"* (I John 4:17).

Our warfare is in the heavenly places and if we are not living out of the heavenly realm, we will never win the heavenly war. The enemy is always trying to bring the church down to the level of the soul (intellect, feelings and opinions) because he knows that they can never defeat him (the enemy) on this level. We are commanded to be strong against the evil one. Our strength is only in the Lord, and the power of His might (Ephesians 6:10). Paul states specifically that we are corporately wrestling principalities, powers, rulers of the darkness, and spiritual forces in high (heavenly) places (Ephesians 6:12).

Every individual is joined to Adam by natural birth and in Adam all die (I Corinthians 15:22). When someone is reborn, they have now joined themselves to the Lord (I Corinthians 6:17) and in their spirit they are united with the resurrected and exalted Christ (I Corinthians 15:21, 22).

Am I living as a Christian in my own strength? Do I see my life as something that I must do? Paul makes a very strong statement against believers who were living as if they were just mere men.

> *"I could not speak to you as unto spiritual men, but as unto carnal (fleshly), even as unto babes in Christ. I have fed you with milk, and not with meat: for until now ye were not able to bear it, neither yet now are ye able. For ye are yet carnal: (fleshly) for whereas there is among you envying, and strife, and divisions, are ye not carnal, and walk as men?"*
>
> I Corinthians 3:1-3

Paul was shocked that these new creations in Christ joined to his ascended Spirit, were living their lives as if they were still natural normal men. It grieves the Spirit of God when his children walk in the natural realm and live as natural mere men instead of walking in the heavenly sphere as sons of God.

Manfrel Haller says, "*For even as the body is one and yet has many members, and all the members of the body, though they are many, are one body, so also is Christ" (I Corinthians 12:12). It´s amazing how little thought is given to this verse, what is revealed from it should take our breath away. One sometimes gets the impression that a lot of Bible reading is done these days, but very little meditation on what is read. The first rule for interpreting the scriptures today is not the text itself, but the generally accepted interpretation of various Christian circles. What a verse means is what our own understanding allows it to mean. Otherwise, I can´t explain why this statement hasn't created a furor long ago. Either Paul has clearly gone too far here, or we simply do not take the Scriptures seriously anymore, because what we read in this passage is downright hair-raising. Just as the human body consists of many components or members, and all belong to a single body, so is Christ!*

"God´s goal, Christ as all and in all", Manfred Haller

I wholeheartedly endorse this statement by Brother Haller. So many times, we read the Scriptures but we think, we analyze, we see what our Christian groups feel, we check out theological viewpoints, and then we make a decision if we should receive the Word just as the Lord God spoke it! This way of thinking has brought Christianity down to just another religion with a set of beliefs to live by. So much of our Christian living today does not need the supernatural presence and power of the living God in order to survive. Many times the natural realm becomes more relevant to a believer than the supernatural even though the Lord has boldly declared, *"Not by might or by power, but by my Spirit"* (Zechariah 4:6). Beloved, have we sold our birthright to walk with the living God? Have we settled for nice churches and nice meeting places that function decently and in order? One of the main Scriptures that reveal the heavenly nature of the church; which is the body of Christ is found in Hebrews 12:22-25)

"But ye are come unto Mount Zion, and unto the city of the living God, the heavenly Jerusalem, and to an innumerable company of angels, To the general assembly and church of the firstborn, which are written in heaven, and to God the Judge of all, and to the spirits of just men made perfect, And to Jesus the mediator of the new covenant, and to the blood of sprinkling, that speaketh better things than that of Abel. See that ye refuse not him that speaketh. For if they escaped not who refused him that spake on earth, much more shall not we escape, if we turn away from him that speaketh from heaven."

This is a description of what is happening when believers gather together. Is this not truly amazing! When we join with the body of Christ; His life, His members, His blood, His angels, His Father and His ever speaking voice are then also joined with us! This is what the Bible refers to as going to church. It is not going to a building where Christians gather. It is experiencing eternal life now and *"tasting the heavenly gift, and trusting the good word of God, and trusting the powers of the age to come"* (Hebrews 6:5-6). Beloved, we do not have to just settle for religion, not when the Lord is offering us reality.

Man has Rejected His Calling

So often when someone considers Enoch, they consider him as attaining something so extremely high and special, a something that no one else could ever attain. Scripture says that Enoch walked with God (Genesis 5:24). But apparently the key to Enoch's walk with God was his faith (Hebrews 11:5, 6). Also, Elias (Elijah) is considered an amazing person and often again, the thought comes that no one could ever experience what he did. But, the Word of God says that, *"Elias was a man subject to like passions as we are," (the same as we are).* (James 5:17).

Is it possible that religion has caused us to focus so much on our self that we have no more faith like David in what the LORD can do through an ordinary vessel. God Almighty is seeking anyone whose heart is loyal and honest towards Him, so that He can show His tremendous power through that one (II Chronicles 16:9).

Jesus got some religious people very angry one day because He declared Himself to be the Son of God and that He and the Father were one (John 10:31-33). Now, let's read what Jesus replies to them.

> *"Jesus answered them, Is it not written in your law, I said, Ye are gods? If he called them gods, unto whom the word of God came, and the scripture cannot be broken; Say ye of him, whom the Father hath sanctified, and sent into the world, Thou blasphemest; because I said, I am the Son of God?"*
>
> John 10:34-36

What an astounding response to the religious people. Jesus was quoting directly from Psalms 82:2-7:

> *"How long will ye judge unjustly, and accept the persons of the wicked? Selah. Defend the poor and fatherless: do justice to the afflicted and needy. Deliver the poor and*

> *needy: rid them out of the hand of the wicked. They know not, neither will they understand; they walk on in darkness: all the foundations of the earth are out of course. I have said, Ye are gods; and all of you are children of the most High. But ye shall die like men, and fall like one of the princes."*

Jesus was rebuking the religious leaders because they were so upset that Jesus declared Himself to be one with God and one in whom the Father lived. He immediately quotes the Word that declares their own destiny to be a vessel for God, to reveal the very nature of God, to defend the poor and needy. This scripture is very clear, our calling as creations of the living eternal God and Father is to manifest Him, to exalt Him, and reveal Him to all people. Like the people referred to in Psalm 82, and the christians in Corinth, we could die as mere men, and totally miss our destiny as children of the Most High God!

Many years ago, with the revelation of this truth, I made a decision that by God's grace I would not die as a mere man, but I would fulfill my purpose in life. Like David, I want to fulfill my purpose for my generation (Acts 13:36).

The prophet Micah said that *"He hath shewed thee, O man, what is good; and what doth the LORD require of thee, but to do justly, and to love mercy, and to walk humbly with thy God?"* (Micah 6:8). In other words, God actually requires us to walk with Him. This is not something extremely special for a people that are extremely special. This is for very ordinary people like us. We must only deal with our pride, because the Lord hates pride, and proud people can never walk with God. The Lord stands afar off from the proud and He also resists the proud. (See author's other books).

Earthly or Heavenly?

There is a demonic, natural wisdom that I can be walking in if there is selfish ambition in my heart (James 3:13-17, Philippians 1:15-17) (See authors book, "Whose Image and Which Mind"). This corrupted, defiled wisdom was first found in satan when he destroyed his wisdom, which was God's wisdom in him. He exalted himself by beholding his own beauty and splendor. Satan´s brightness and perfection caused his heart to be lifted up on the inside and this destroyed the wisdom with which he was created by God (Ezekiel 28:12, 17). If the heart of the Lamb is inside of a believer; there will be no selfish ambition, and heavenly wisdom will be poured into his heart.

If there is a secret desire to get the applause and recognition of others, then there will be an earthy demonic wisdom with confusion and it will accompany this person wherever they go (James 3:14-16). Heavenly wisdom pours into a heart that is pure without any hidden desire to be exalted by others. This person´s life will be accompanied by peace and gentleness (James 3:17-18). If a Christian is living out of the earthly realm; then he or she is probably depending on their own understanding to solve problems and to make decisions. Once again, God is very clear when He tells us to not lean on our own understanding, but in all of our ways trust in Him and He will direct our steps (Proverbs 3:5, 6). Intellectual pride can be a great hindrance to knowing God´s mind and doing his will. If a person is living out of the heavenly realm; then they are listening to the anointing that is deep within their spirit and it is teaching them "all things" (I John 2:20, 27). "But ye have an unction from the Holy One, and ye know *all things.*" *"But the anointing which ye have received of him abideth in you, and ye need not that any man teach you: but as the same anointing teacheth you of all things, and is truth, and is no lie, and even as it hath taught you, ye shall abide in him."* In the natural realm we live by our intellect, but in the heavenly realm we live by the anointing that teaches us everything.

In the natural realm there is an earthly love. This earthly love gives an appearance of a real and pure love. That is until someone disagrees, rebukes, or offends the person in earthly love. Now, the true attitude of the heart will manifest in the form of retaliation, anger, self-pity, judgment, criticism, and hardness. If someone is living in the heavenly realm then they are depending on the Holy Spirit to pour the love of God into them and through them for others. (Romans 5:5). There is an enormous difference between God´s pure love and man´s impure selfish love. God needs no reason to love, except simply that it is his very nature. Human love will love someone until they get upset and hurt their feelings. God´s pure love will cause a husband to see his wife in a totally different way and also it will cause a wife to see her husband in a totally different way. When someone looks through the eyes of God, they will look at people with eyes of compassion. Although, when someone looks at someone with the natural eyes from the earthly realm they will see the mistakes and the things that the other person could do better.

Beloved the Holy Spirit is calling the Bride, calling her to come up higher and begin to live in the heavenly realm. Desiring that his Bride not die as a mere men! Do not sell your birthright, which is the privilege of walking with God as one of his sons!

CHAPTER 6

THINE IS THE GLORY!

"I am the LORD: that is my name: and my glory will I not give to another, neither my praise to graven images."

Isaiah 42:8

"For thine is the kingdom, and the power, and the glory, forever. Amen."

Matthew 6:13

"Saying with a loud voice, Worthy is the Lamb that was slain to receive power, and riches, and wisdom, and strength, and honour, and glory, and blessing. And every creature which is in heaven, and on the earth, and under the earth, and such as are in the sea, and all that are in them, heard I saying, Blessing, and honour, and glory, and power, be unto him that sitteth upon the throne, and unto the Lamb forever and ever."

Revelation 5:12, 13

All of creation was called to reveal the image of the One that created it, and to glorify the LORD GOD ALMIGHTY and to praise and honor him. He is the only God and there is no Savior besides Him. From the beginning of creation, it was the Father´s plan to have a man that would receive his very life and have dominion over every living creature. Men were supposed to eat from the tree of life and live forever; but he had to choose. From the very beginning, God was to be his supply. The Lamb was slain before the foundations of the world. God provided a solution to man's problem even before man knew he had a problem. From the very beginning the Father's solution was his Son for all of mankind's problems

The Lord made a covenant with Abram right in the beginning of Genesis. In a covenant, there are two parties and each party is obligated to walk through the pieces of a dead animal. In this Abrahamic covenant, a smoking oven and a flaming torch walked through the pieces for Abram (Genesis 15:17, 18) because Abram was asleep. We are told that there is a rest for the people of God (Hebrews 4). He that enters into the Father's rest ceases from his own works (Hebrews 4:10). God put Abram to sleep (rest) while this flaming torch walked through the pieces of the animal. Who was this smoking furnace and flaming torch? We discover in (Daniel 10:6) and (Revelation 1:13, 14) that this One was the Lord Jesus Christ in his pre-incarnate state that passed through the pieces. The One that walked through the pieces to make a covenant for Abram is the same one that walked through the pieces for us all.

There is an eternal principle that must never be broken. We find this in Romans 11:35-36 *"Who hath first given to him, and it shall be recompensed unto him again? For of him, and through him, and to him, are all things: to whom be glory forever. Amen."* No one first gives to God. The source is always God. This is why the

Lord will not and cannot share His glory with another. His glory means that *all* the power, *all* the credit, *all* the honor and *all* the ability comes from the Lord. He is the originator, the sustainer and the fulfiller. He is the Sovereign Lord and the credit always belongs to Him. Coming out of Him, and through Him and back to Him are *all things* forever. Therefore, to Him be all the glory now and forever.

For example, if someone gets saved it is because God's grace caused someone to pray and then God´s grace came to the person in response to prayer and enabled them to receive Jesus. Revival also begins with the Holy Spirit placing a burden on someone and then He gives the grace necessary to pray in travail for revival. Next, the Holy Spirit comes upon a person or a group and empowers them to witness and then the Presence and power get stronger and there is more grace to pray and intercede and therefore more of the miraculous presence of God in that place. From start to finish, the grace of God comes and enables God´s will and purposes to be accomplished. What is man´s part? Man's part is to ask, expect and appropriate the grace and mercy of God, ultimately to accomplish the purpose of God.

When it is understood that no one first gives to God, then all of the provision of God is received by faith and from start to finish it is a work of grace. Some people who are praying for revival will never experience revival because they are focused on their praying instead of God´s grace. When we focus on what we must do instead of the grace of God that enables me to do it, I am taking the credit to my goodness instead of giving the credit to God´s glory.

One of the main ways that a person touches the glory of God is by judging others. Whenever we judge others, it is usually because in our hearts we feel that we are not like them because of our own achievements and goodness (Romans 2:1, 14:10, 12).

The eternal truth is that we can only stand by the grace of God (I Corinthians 15:10). When we make judgments out of our pride, then the Lord must remove His grace from that area in our life.

God´s glory is tied in to his ability, and my glory comes out of all that I am boasting of in myself. I am rejoicing in my own ability, and this is becomes my glory. One could say that my glory is related to my ability and God's glory is related to his ability. He must receive the glory, because He alone is the One who accomplishes all things for us. *"Lord, thou wilt ordain peace for us: for thou also hast wrought all our works in us"* (Isaiah 26:12). *"Being confident of this very thing, that he which has begun a good work in you will perform it until the day of Jesus Christ"* (Philippians 1:6). *"Faithful is he who calls you, who also will do it"* (Thessalonians 5:24). Jesus said, "Whatsoever you ask in my name, that will I do, that the Father may be glorified in the Son" (John 14:13).

God as the Origin of All Things

There are many examples in the Bible of the significance that God is the originator of all things. *"When his disciples heard it, they were exceedingly amazed, saying, 'Who then can be saved?' But Jesus beheld them, and said unto them, 'With men this is impossible; but with God all things are possible' "* (Matthew 19:25, 26). Jesus is telling his disciples that it is impossible with men and therefore God is necessary to accomplish everything. Why did Jesus declare this is impossible with men? *"And Jesus answered and said unto him, Blessed art thou, Simon Barjona: for flesh and blood hath not revealed it unto thee, but my Father which is in heaven"* (Matthew 16:17). Jesus is warning Peter not take the credit to himself, but instead to understand that this was the grace of God that allowed him to understand this.

> *"From that time forth began Jesus to shew unto his disciples, how that he must go unto Jerusalem, and suffer many things of the elders and chief priests and scribes, and be killed, and be raised again the third day. Then Peter took him, and began to rebuke him, saying, 'Be it far from thee, Lord: this shall not be unto thee.' But he turned, and said unto Peter, 'Get thee behind me, Satan: thou art not mindful of the things of God, but those that be of men' "*
>
> *Matthew 16:21-23*

Jesus had tried to warn Peter about the danger of his pride, but he did not have ears to hear. Here we see how Peter allows the devil to use his mind and speak through his lips because he did not understand that the glory is the Lord's. Even in the case of revelation; this is not something that a person can get apart from the Lord showing it to them. *"And if any man think that he knows anything, he knows nothing yet as he ought to know."* (1 Corinthians 8:2). We learn the things of the Spirit through revelation and not by information. Peter thought that he was so committed to God that he would even die with Jesus. Jesus again warns him and tells him that he is going to fall, because the devil is going to knock him down. Once again, Peter did not heed Jesus' warning (Luke 22:31-34). (missing something connect to next paragraph)

An amazing example of God being the originator of spiritual things is found in Matthew 9:36-38, *"But when he saw the multitudes, he was moved with compassion on them, because they fainted, and were scattered abroad, as sheep having no shepherd. Then saith he unto his disciples, the harvest is plenteous, but the laborers are few; pray ye therefore the Lord of the harvest, that he will send forth laborers into his harvest."* Even in view of a plenteous harvest waiting to be picked, it is necessary to pray that the Lord will send out workers. Why not just go out and bring in the fruit? Why, because it must have its origin in God alone. *"Of Him, and through Him and to Him are all things, to whom be the glory forever"* (Romans 11:36). *"All things are delivered to me of my Father; and no man knoweth the Son, but the Father, neither knoweth any man the Father; except the Son, and he to whomsoever the Son will reveal him."* (Matthew 11:27). Here again we see that the Lord must reveal Himself to man. *"It is not of the will of man, but the will of God"* (John 1:13). Only the grace of God can enable one to make th right choices in life. *"No man can come to me, except the Father which hath sent me draw him"* (John 6:44). Again, we are told by Jesus how totally dependent we are on the grace of God.

Now, let us read about the man after God's own heart, David. *"Give unto the Lord, o ye mighty, give unto the Lord glory and strength. Give unto the Lord the glory due unto his name; worship the Lord in the beauty of holiness"* (Psalm 29:1, 2). David is saying that the mighty people on earth should give the Lord all the praise, because all their strength comes from Him. *"Thine, O Lord, is the greatness, and the power, and the glory, and the victory, and the majesty; for all that is in the heaven and in the earth is thine: thine is the kingdom, O Lord, and thou art exalted as head above all. Both riches and honour come of thee, and thou reignest over all; and in thine hand is power and might; and in thine hand it is to make great, and to give strength to all. Now, therefore, our God, we thank thee, and praise thy glorious name. But who am I, and what is my people, that we should be able to offer so willingly after this sort? For all things come out of thee, and of thine own have we given thee. O Lord our God, all this store that we have prepared to build thee an house for thine holy name comes out of thine and is all thine own!"*

I Choronicles 29:11-16

David so greatly pleased the Father and yet he said that his sins were so numerous that he could not count them all. It was his heart attitude that was so extremely precious to the Father. David also had a deep understanding that all the glory goes to God for everything. David even said that all that he *could* glory in would give the Lord alone praise. The Lord is looking for people who want to show the world what He can do for them, in them and through them. The Lord at this time is raising up a Davidic generation of people who are true worshippers and warriors. Their main passion will be to give glory to the great and majestic name of the Lord. They will yearn to live only for His name's sake! They will deeply understand that all comes from him and that He governs all nations by his supreme power.

Kings that did not understand the sovereign rule of the Lord

KING SENNACHERIB

King Sennacherib boasted of all his victories over all the nations and their gods. Now, he was threatening King Hezekiah that he would demolish him also like he did to the other rulers. The Lord said to tell King Sennacherib, *"Hast thou not heard long ago how I have done it, and of ancient times that I have formed it? now have I brought it to pass, that thou should be to lay waste fenced cities into ruinous heaps"* (2 Kings 19:25).

In other words, the Lord was notifying King Sennacherib that all of his success was due to the fact that the Sovereign Lord allowed it. Now, since he was boasting against his Maker, that very night he and his army were destroyed.

KING NEBUCHADNEZZAR

Daniel warned King Nebuchadnezzar to turn from his pride and maybe God would have mercy, but he refused to repent. Therefore, God deals with his pride by sending him into insanity and seven years of judgment. Then, King Nebuchadnezzar says at the end of seven years, *"Now, I Nebuchadnezzar praise and extol and honour the King of heaven, all whose works are truth, and his ways judgment; and those who walk in pride he is able to abase"* (Daniel 4:37).

KING HEROD

King Herod simply gives a speech and the people say that it is the voice of a god and not a man and immediately God kills King Herod (Acts 12:21-23). We are told why he was killed and it was because he did not give the glory to the Lord (vs. 23).

PHARAOH

Pharaoh said who is the Lord that I should obey him (Exodus 5:2)? This one statement led to the total destruction of Pharaoh and his entire empire!

My dear brothers and sisters, this issue about the glory of God is not a secondary issue. It is of the highest and greatest importance. The Lord will not give His glory to another or to any graven image. There shall be no other gods and none other shall receive the praise and glory that the Lord alone deserves. Brothers and sisters, do we give the honor and glory to the God who uses a vessel or do we give glory to the vessel that God uses? The Lord must raise up the tabernacle of David in the last days because there must be a people who will not want to touch God's glory and they will walk in the revelation of all that Christ is and that Christ is all! It does not say that Christ gives all, but that Christ is all! He himself is all within the body. He himself is the

Life, the Way, the Truth and everything else. Truly, all the glory belongs to his great and glorious name. We must continue to pursue the issue of the glory of God. I feel to repeat that when I use the term glory, I am referring to the credit and honor that is only due to the name of the Lord. The reason for this is because *"of Him, and through Him, and to Him are all things, to whom be glory forever"* (Romans 11:36).

When we start to understand this all-important subject of God's glory; then we will begin to apprehend why Christ must be all within the church; which is his body. Andrew Murray says, "Look up and see the infinite God waiting to do everything as soon as we are ready to give up all to Him, and receive all from Him" (Andrew Murray; The Two Covenants, January 2004 Bethel Baptist Print Ministry).

Beloved, to finally come to the truth that I, like Jesus, can do nothing out of myself is not to encourage laziness and passivity. Instead, a door is now wide open to see all that God will do in me and through me. To say that I can do nothing out of my own ability is not saying that I will do nothing; it is only declaring that I can do nothing and therefore, I will let the Holy Spirit do all in me. He will write the law on my heart and in my mind. He will circumcise my heart to love God completely and most of all He will reveal the risen Christ in me, to me and through me. I firmly believe that one reason the good news of the gospel is for the needy, poor and the weak is because these are the only ones that truly see how much they need God. The people that the Lord is using to raise up the former desolations of many past generations are the poor, the afflicted, the broken-hearted and the captives (Isaiah 64:1-4).

> *"But God has chosen the foolish things of the world to confound the wise; and God has chosen the weak things of*

the world to confound the things which are mighty. And base things of the world, and things which are despised hath God chosen, yea and things which are not, to bring to nothing things that are; that no flesh should glory in his presence. But of him are ye in Christ Jesus, who of God is made to us wisdom, and righteousness, and sanctification, and redemption, that, according as it is written, He that glorieth, let him glory in the Lord"

1 Corinthians 1:27-31

Everything and everyone, that men glory in other than Jesus Christ, will be removed in the great shaking that is now taking place around the world (Isaiah 2 and Hebrews 12:27-29). All the little ones that are nothing in their own eyes, God is raising out of the dust to sit with kings and princes (Psalm 113:7, 8). The Lord delights to give beauty for ashes (Isaiah 61:3). When there are ashes, there is nothing left to burn! These are people who have nothing left of themself. They have come to the end of themselves and now they can truly put no more confidence in the flesh.

Through the blood of the Lamb, the Father has raised up the Shepherd and Bishop of our souls. And through the same blood of the New Covenant, the Father is causing this Risen Christ through the Spirit to live in and through each of his members.

"Now, the God of peace, that brought again from the dead our Lord Jesus, that great Shepherd of the sheep, through the blood of the everlasting covenant, make you perfect in every good work to do his will, working in you that which is well-pleasing in his sight, through Jesus Christ; to whom be glory forever and ever, Amen!"

Hebrews 13, 20, 21

Likewise, in Peter's epistle we read, "If any man speak, let him speak as the oracles of God; if any man serve, let him do it as of the ability which God gives; that God in all things may be glorified through Jesus, Christ, to whom be praise and dominion forever and ever Amen" (1 Peter 4:11). Now, is the time for a Jesus without mixture; not human goodness trying to live like Jesus, but Jesus Christ coming into an empty vessel, that truly believes they can do nothing out of themselves. It is now time for God to be glorified in *all* things!

The Lie: A need to be strong

When a person sees their own weakness then they will see how much they need the grace of God. One main obstacle to allowing the mighty God to live through me is my own sense that I must be strong. Many have been raised in families that did not allow them to make mistakes or to show weakness. This creates within a child a fear of being weak and a constant attempt at being strong. As life continues, one will learn to do more and more out of their own natural abilities. Beloved, it might do good to just ask yourself the question, do I rejoice in the areas where I am weak? If I am rejoicing in the areas that I am strong and capable; then what do I need God for? Like King Uzziah, God will marvelously help me until I am strong (1 Chronicles 26: 13-16). But, if I, like the Apostle Paul am rejoicing in my weaknesses, then God will show Himself strong in my weakness (2 Corinthians 12:7-10).

The Father's Secret Way

There is a secret mystery hidden in the very bosom of the Father's heart. This is the mystery of the Lamb slain (John 1:14, 18). The Seed had to be sown into death in order that His uncreated, eternal life could be released throughout his entire body. Every seed has to bear fruit after its own kind and the incorruptible seed called the Word of God had to reproduce its own kind into the hearts of believers.

> *"Being born again, not, of corruptible seed, but of incorruptible, by the Word of God, which lives and abides forever. For all flesh is as grass, and all the glory of man as the flower of grass. The grass withers, and the flower therof falleth away. But the Word of the Lord endureth forever. And this is the Word which by the gospel is preached to you"*
>
> 1 Peter 1:23-25

> *"Whereof, I am made a minister, according to the dispensation of God which is given to me for you, to fulfill the word of God. Even the mystery which has been hid from ages and from generations, but now is being manifested to his saints, to whom God would make known what is the riches of the glory of this mystery among the Gentiles, which is Christ in you; the hope of glory"*
>
> Colossians 1:25, 27

The first Person of the Godhead, God the Father, has given the second person of the Godhead to come and triumph in every dimension and every area. *"There are three that bear record in heaven, the Father, the Word and the Holy Ghost and these three are one" (1 John 5:7). "The Word was made flesh and dwelt amongst us. And we beheld his glory, the glory as of the only begotten of the Father, full of grace and truth" (John 1:14). "That which was from the beginning, which we have heard, which we have seen, with our eyes, which we have looked upon, and our hands have handled, of the Word of Life was manifested, and we have seen it, and bear witness, and shew unto you that eternal life, which was with the Father, and was manifested unto us" (1 John 1:1, 2). "But the Word of God grew and multiplied" (Acts 12:24).*

Now is the time for the Father to reveal the Word in fullness. This dispensation of God will bring to fullness the revelation and manifestation of a living Person. The Word became flesh and the same Word has been sown into the hearts of every member of His body. This Word has character, he has life, HE is the Creator, He is the light and in Him is no darkness at all. This mystery of the pre-incarnate Christ has been buried in the very bosom of the Father, but now has been manifested in all of his fullness, grace and glory. The Word is not just something to declare; but it is also someone to manifest. Paul refers to this as "the manifestation of the truth" (2 Corinthians 4:2). Jesus said, *"I am the Way, the Truth and the Life"* (John 14:6). Jesus does not give us or show us the way. He is the way. He is the total truth and He is the very life. He himself is all that we need. In him is found the fullness of the Godhead. *"In him dwelleth all the fullness of the Godhead bodily"* (Colossians 2:9). *"For it pleased the Father that in him should all the fullness dwell"* (Colossians 1:19).

Dear ones, the Father has given us His dear Son to be for us, in us and through us all that we could ever need. Let's imagine for a moment, that there was a city, but there was only one way to get inside of that city and it was through a tunnel. No airplane, no other route or way could take a person into that city. It was through a secret tunnel. Once the tunnel was discovered; then the way was found and any person could then enjoy the beauty that the city contained. All the riches of that city could be experienced and enjoyed once the secret tunnel was discovered.

Dear brothers and sisters, Jesus is the rest that remains for the people of God. He himself is the promised land of God's fullness. Canaan does not represent heaven, because if it did, this would mean that Moses is in hell. No, Canaan is a land of rest and Christ is the Sabbath rest for the people of God (Hebrews 4:7-16). Jesus is the Way and the life and the Truth. Jesus is our redeemer, our mercy seat, our righteousness, our strength, our sanctification, our redemption. The Father has made him to be all in all to his body (1 Corinthians 1:30, 31; Ephesians 1:22, 23; Colossians 3:11, John 14:6, Psalm 18, Romans 3:25) and many more. *"For if, when we were enemies, we were reconciled to God by the death of his Son, much more, being reconciled, we shall be saved by his life"* (Romans 5:10). *"For if by one man's offence death reigned by one; much more they which receive abundance of grace and of the gift of righteousness shall reign in life by one, Jesus Christ"* (Roman 5:17). We are called to rule and reign in this life through the very risen life of the exalted Son of God. What a glorious gospel we have in Christ which is the victorious message through Christ living in us.

If we try to experience abundant life, but we never find the secret way; then we could suffer many, many disappointments. There is a key word that Paul so often uses in his writings and it is the word 'through'. This key word shows us the secret tunnel into the fullness of God. If I am trying to experience revival, but my trust is based on my commitment, my devotion and my fasting; then I will miss the secret mystery of God; which is Christ. *"How that by revelation he made known unto me the mystery; as I wrote above in a few words, Whereby, when ye read, ye many understand my knowledge in the mystery of Christ"* (Ephesians 3:3-4).

Christ is the secret to experiencing Revival and not an experience. Christ Jesus is the secret to peace and not an experience or a feeling. Jesus Christ is the mystery or the secret channel to all the fullness of the riches of the Father for his children. It is not another program, or another sermon or another way. It is

Jesus himself as the way. Let us read some Scriptures that use this tremendously important word; through.

> *"Nay in all these things we are more than conquerors through him that loved us"*
>
> Romans 8:37

> *"For of him and through him and to him are all things; to whom be glory forever, Amen"*
>
> Romans 11:36

> *"But thanks be to God, which giveth us the victory through our Lord Jesus Christ (1Corinthians 15:57). "Make you perfect in every good work to do his will, working in you that which is well pleasing in his sight, through Jesus Christ; to whom be glory forever and ever" (Hebrews 13:21). "In this was manifested the love of God toward us, because that God sent his only begotten Son into the world, that we might live through him"*
>
> 1 John 4:9

God is constantly giving everyone who will receive it, the victory *through* Jesus (1 Corinthians 15:57). Through the Son are all things for ever and ever (Romans 11:36). This includes a fantastic marriage, victory, revival, humility, the radiant presence of Christ and all that we need. We are always conquerors through the very Son of God, no matter what we are going through. If I am trying to conquer through my devotion or prayer life; it will not happen because then the Father would have to take the glory off himself and give it to me. If I can overcome through me, then I must get the credit or glory for what I have done! But, the truth is that my God and your God shall supply all of our needs according to his glorious riches in His Son (Philippians 4:19). Jesus Christ through us is that secret Way into the fullness of God.

Thine is Always the Glory!

Lucifer was created so beautiful, so brilliant and so perfect that he thought it was due to something inside of him. In other words, Lucifer took the glory that belonged to Jehovah and rejoiced in all the beauty that he could see in himself. He actually thought that he himself was the source of his beauty and perfection. *"Thine heart was lifted up because of thine beauty, thou hast corrupted thy wisdom by reason of thy brightness"* (Ezekiel 28:17a). It was Lucifer's beauty and perfection that was his downfall. So many times we think that our weakness, insufficiency and lack leads to our downfall. It is actually our riches, success and beauty that usually leads to our downfall.

Men were created to be completed by God's abundance. Love never seeks its own; therefore the very nature of God, which is love, is constantly seeking someone to pour Himself into. He, as pure love, can never be satisfied until He pours himself into another (1 Corinthians 13:5, 1 John 4:12). One could almost say that God made us so that we could only be completed and fulfilled through and by Him. There is a God shaped void in every person and only God Himself can fill to our great satisfaction.

The original sin is man's erroneous thinking that makes him believe that he can be his own god; independent of the true God and the true vine (John 17:3, 15:1). Independence is a major curse that is on the human race. We humans were never supposed to be independent. Our true calling is to be a vessel that is filled with all the fullness of God himself (Ephesians 3:19, 4:13). The

Lord spoke to Ezekiel an analogy about his children and this is very appropriate also to most of us that have found Christ as our Savior. Ezekiel 16:

"And say, Thus saith the Lord God unto Jerusalem; thy birth and thy nativity is of the land of Canaan, thy father was an Amorite, and thy mother was a Hittite (we also were born into the race of Adam). *"And as for thy nativity, in the day thou wast born thy navel was not cut, neither wast thou washed in water to supple thee; thou wast not salted at all, nor swaddled at all, none eye pitied thee, to do any of these things to thee, to have compassion on thee; but thou wast cast out in the open field, to the loathing of thy person, in the day thou wast born"* (so many people are brought up into a world with no love and no compassion, they learn to live for themselves and to take care of themself). *"And when I passed by thee, and saw thee polluted in thy own blood. I said to thee when thou wast polluted in thy blood, live; yea I said unto thee when thou was in thy blood, live!"* (The Lord spoke His creative word and we came alive for the first time.) *"I have caused thee to multiply as the bud of the field, and thou hast increased and waxen great, and thou art come to excellent ornaments, thy breasts are fashioned, and thine hair is grown, whereas thou wast naked and bare"* (most people that are saved experience a radical transformation whereby they clean up their life and all of a sudden life now has meaning for them after they are re-born). *"Now, when I passed by thee, and looked upon thee, behold, thy time was the time of love, and I spread my skirt over thee, and covered thy nakedness: yea, I swore unto thee and entered into a covenant with thee, saith the Lord God, and thou became mine"* (Next, we enter into a love covenant with the precious Redeemer and we see ourselves as belonging just to Him). *"Then I washed thee with water; yea, I thoroughly washed away they blood from thee, and I anointed thee with oil"* (first, the Lord cleanses us and then he anoints us). *"I clothed thee also with*

broidered work, and shod thee with badger's skin, and I girded thee about with fine linen, and I covered thee with silk. I decked thee also with ornaments, and I put bracelets upon thy hands, and a chain on thy neck. And I put a jewel on thy forehead, and earrings in thine ears, and a beautiful crown upon thine head". "Thus was thou decked with gold and silver; and thy raiment was of fine linen, and silk, and broidered work; thou didst eat fine flour, and honey, and oil; and thou wast exceedingly beautiful, and thou didst prosper into a kingdom" (Next, the Holy Spirit gives gifts to his children; he anoints them and gives them special things that beautify them more and more). With the gifts, the anointings, the blessings and the abundance of love; the people of God will grow stronger and stronger in numbers, beauty and power. This is when the danger comes. In the success, the pride in the heart of men will look at all that the Lord has done in them, for them and through them; but they start to see themselves as the very source of their blessings and they take the glory away from the Lord and put it on themself. *"And thy renown went forth among the heathen for thy beauty; for it was perfect through my comeliness, which I had put upon thee, saith the Lord" "But, then didst trust in thine own beauty, and played the harlot because of thy renown"* (Ezekiel 16:3-14).

Throughout the last four or five thousand years, men have not been able to handle success when the Lord God gives it to them. This issue about the glory of God is a main issue for this hour within Christendom. The Lord must have a people now who He can use and work through them, but they will acknowledge that truly this is the Lord Himself and it is marvelous in our eyes! Then the earth will be filled with the knowledge of the glory of the Lord. We are just vessels, therefore we can be a vessel for God or we can be a vessel for the evil one. We read in Romans 6:19 that to whomsoever we yield ourselves to obey, to that one we become his vessel. Peter was a vessel for Father God and satan within a few moments time (Matthew 16:16, 22, 23). There is so much revelation of man's glory that the knowledge of God's glory is being blocked in so many ways. However, the Davidic generation is being birthed with a deep passion to give Him the glory due his name. So be it Lord Jesus! At the end of time all of creation will only behold the glory of God and no one will question whose glory it is. Therefore at this time there is a people prepared to be a vessel for the glory of God. If I will be part of this vessel, then I must lose my glory; which is my image in this world. His glory and His image will replace our glory and our image. Our prayer is: come now with all of Your glory and may Your image be seen in Your body. Amen!

CHAPTER 7

THE ALL INCLUSIVE CHRIST

As I am writing this chapter, I am at a hotel and my wife and I have purchased the all-inclusive package. Basically, this means that we pay one price and included in this price is everything that we will need. The Father has given us His Son and included in the gift of His Son is everything that we need! In Christ is a dimension that we are called to live. Within this heavenly realm we will have discernment by his Spirit; experience his pure love, revival, cleansing, redemption, wisdom, righteousness, life, truth, holiness, humility and everything that we need for life and godliness.

> *"Grace and peace be multiplied unto you through the knowledge of God, and of Jesus our Lord, according as his divine power has given to us all things, that pertain to life and godliness through the knowledge of him that hath called us to glory and virtue" "Whereby are given unto us exceeding great and precious promises; that by these ye*

might be partakers of the divine nature having escaped the corruption that is in the world through lusts"

2 Peter 1:2-4

In the new covenant, Christ, as our High Priest and Surety will be all we need to fulfill the covenant (Hebrews 3:1, 7:20, 22, 25). If a person will give everything over to Christ; then Christ will have the full responsibility to create a heart that is totally pleasing to the Father. Christ himself will abide and dwell within the heart and He will fill the whole being with his perfect love and perfect life (Ephesians 3:17:19). He will even quicken the mortal bodies by his Spirit (Romans 8:11). No one is able to overcome and to keep themselves. We need Christ to be our constant keeper. *"Now unto him that is able to keep you faultless before the presence of his glory with exceeding joy"* (Jude 1:24). God, the Father has placed us in his Son and in this realm, Christ becomes everything to his body. *"But of him are ye in Christ Jesus, who of God is made to us wisdom, and righteousness, and sanctification, and redemption. That, according as it is written, He that glorieth, let him glory in the Lord"* (1 Corinthians 1:30, 31).

Christ is the beginning of the new creation or the new humanity. In this new humanity, there are new types of persons, ones who will please God with their lives. The old creation or humanity can never please God for as Paul said those in the flesh cannot please God (Romans 8:8). The cross is God's verdict on the old creation: a death sentence. God has sentenced the old humanity to death so that he could raise up a new humanity. (2 Cor. 1:9) The Bible calls this new humanity a new creation in Christ. The cross is the end of the old and the resurrection is the beginning of the new. In the scriptures, Christ is called the last Adam and the second Man. The last Adam refers to the end of the old Adamic race. The second Man is the beginning of the new creation in Christ (I Cor. 15:45, 47). The Father's complete and perfect work has been accomplished in His Son and all that pleases the Father's heart is what His Son has done, is doing and will do. *"For by one offering he hath perfected forever them that are sanctified"* (Hebrews 10:14).

The Apostle Paul, when he was Saul, opposed everything that Jesus Christ stood for. There was a vicious hatred in his pharisaical heart towards Jesus and his followers. But afterwards, the Holy Spirit revealed the mystery of Christ to Paul and opened his spiritual eyes. He saw some of the greatest revelations of this mystery that is hidden in the Father's heart before the world began.

Deep insights that Paul saw as a result of the Father revealing his Son to him

> *To reveal his Son in me, that I might preach him among the heathen; immediately I conferred not with flesh and blood*
>
> Galatians 1:16

1. Christ was his life (Colossians 3:3, Galatians 2:20; Philippians 1:21).
2. The only thing that matters to the Father is a new creation (Galatians 6:15).
3. Through the cross, the world is crucified to Paul and he is crucified to it As long as one embraces the cross, the power of the world's system cannot touch him.(Galatians 6:14).
4. The Father had an eternal purpose to have a family before Adam was even created (Ephesians 1:4-5).
5. In the fullness of times, the Father will gather together all things in heaven and earth in his Son. Nothing is acceptable outside of the Son. (Ephesians 1:10).

6. The church is the body called to reveal Christ on earth (Ephesians 1:22, 23).
7. The entire body is joined to its head in the heavenly places, seated with the ascended Christ (Ephesians 2:6).
8. There are many riches that are unsearchable regarding the mystery of this glorious Christ (Ephesians 3:8).
9. There is an intimate fellowship with others who are walking in this mystery (Ephesians 3:9).
10. The Father's eternal purpose has been planned to reveal, through the church, his eternal wisdom to the ruling powers in heavenly places (Ephesians 3:10, 11).
11. There is only one family and they are joined together in heaven and on earth and Christ is the substance of all (Ephesians 3:14-17).
12. Christ has ascended, for one major purpose and that is to fill all things with his Spirit (Ephesians 4:10).
13. The Father's heart will never be satisfied until the body is filled with the fullness of his Son (Ephesians 4:13).
14. The church or the body of Christ is joined in combat with the spiritual forces of evil in the heavenly places to enforce the dominion of its Lord on earth. We are to preach the kingdom of God now and expect its power to manifest because the King himself is living in us. (Ephesians 6:12).
15. There is a prize to win, which is referred to as the high-calling in Christ Jesus for all of his body. This prize enables one to live out of the resurrected life of Christ constantly (Philippians 3:11-14).
16. Christ is the first-born of the new creation (Colossians 1:15, Revelations 3:14).
17. Christ is the Creator and all things were created by Him and for Him (Colossians 1:16).

18. All things are held together only by Christ and his almighty Word (Colossians 1:17, Hebrews 1:3).
19. The Father is pleased that all the fullness dwells in His Son (Colossians 1:19).
20. There is suffering that is necessary in order for the body of Christ to come to fullness (Colossians 1:24).
21. As Christians allow their hearts to be knit together in love, they will be brought into the riches of the mystery of God and they will experience great comfort (Colossians 2:2).
22. In Christ are hidden all the treasures of heavenly wisdom and knowledge (Colossians 2:3).
23. A believer has all the fullness by being joined to Christ in spirit and therefore as they walk in this realm of the spirit they can be complete (Colossians 2:10).
24. Paul's calling was to manifest the hidden riches of this glorious mystery of Christ (Colossians 4:4, Colossians 1:27-29).
25. God has saved us and called us with a holy calling before the world began to reveal this mystery of Christ (2 Timothy 1:9, 10).
26. One cannot receive reality by learning, it will only come through revelation that the Holy Spirit gives to us (1 Corinthians 2:14).
27. Paul's desires just to know Christ more and more increased (Philippians 3:8-10).
28. Paul discovered that since Christ was so great and so sufficient, his own weakness was one of his greatest assets (2 Corinthians 12:9-10).
29. Maybe the most inclusive is the revelation that the Spirit gave Paul that Christ is *all and in all* (Colossians 3:11).

This one supreme revelation consumed the apostle Paul's mind, heart and life and he yearned to bring the body into the fullness of the risen Lord. He told his spiritual children, "My little children, of whom I travail in birth again until Christ be formed in you" (Galatians 4:19). Paul went from hating and despising Christ Jesus to loving, adoring and being consumed with the revelation of his Person. Have we seen yet that the Christian life is not about us, but only about Christ? Christ himself is the very essence and substance of the Christian life. Christ is all! Can there be a statement that is anymore all-inclusive than this: Christ is all.

Paul did not say that Christ will *give* all, but He *is* all. It must be stated very clearly that the New Testament Christianity is a risen, exalted person living in his body, walking on earth through his Spirit. Jesus said to his disciples after the resurrection "As the Father has sent me, so I send you; receive the Holy Spirit." Out from His risen self he breathed on them the very life that was his life. The very one that caused him to present his body to his Father as a living sacrifice (Hebrews 9:14). *"Not by might, or by power, but by my Spirit, says the Lord of Hosts"* (Zechariah 4:6). Paul had a tremendous revelation that the exalted Lord became a life-giving Spirit. It is as we are believing in Him; that He breathes into us rivers of life-giving water to flow through us into the entire world (John 7:37-39). Our Lord and Savior has taken into his body everything that could hinder us and prevent us from doing the perfect will of God!

He became sin for us (2 Corinthians 5:21).
He bore our sicknesses in his body (actual meaning)(Isaiah 53:4).
He carried all of our pains in his body (Isaiah 53:4).
He was beaten that we could enjoy peace (Isaiah 53:5).
He took our sorrows (Isaiah 53:3).
He took our wrath and our hell by drinking the cup (Matthew 26:42).

He had all of our iniquity laid on him (Isaiah 53:6).

He became a curse for us (Galatians 3:13).

He was cut off from people, stripped of his dignity and honor so that we could receive favor (Isaiah 53:8).

He destroyed him that had the power of death, which is the devil (Hebrews 2:14).

He made an open spectacle of his conquered foes; the powers of darkness that try to oppress and defeat us (Colossians 2:15).

He nailed every decree against us to his cross and it is now written, *'Pardoned'*! (Colossians 2:14).

He overcame every temptation that the evil one could put against him (Hebrews 2:18).

He experienced total abandonment from God (Psalm 22:1). We never have to allow loneliness to consume us again.

He released complete mercy for all offenders that would receive his gift. He said, "Father forgive them".

The veil in the temple was torn in two and there is no longer a wall of separation between men and God because our high priest has caused the veil to be torn apart (Matthew 27:51).

Jesus Christ became the perfect Lamb, the complete and perfect substitute so that all mankind can now experience the fullness of life through Jesus. He said the thief comes to steal, kill and destroy; but I am come that ye might have life and life in abundance" (John 10:10). Are we now beholding Christ as all or are we beholding something in us that we need. Are we still seeking *something* or have we seen that it is *Someone*?

One day, some followers said to Jesus, "Lord, give us this bread" (John 6:34). The bread of life was standing right in front of them, but they did not have eyes to see. Pilate said, "What is truth?" Truth was standing right in front of him, but he did not have eyes to see.

Beloved, Jesus is saying to us today, just as he said many years ago, *"He that comes to me shall never hunger, and he that believes on me shall never thirst"* (John 6:35). He that believes on the risen Christ shall never, ever thirst or hunger! Also, Jesus told a sinful woman, *"Whosoever drinketh of the water that I shall give him shall never thirst; but the water that I shall give him shall be in him a well of water springing up into everlasting life"* (John 4:14). Jesus, the all-inclusive Christ is offering us today all that we will ever need in life and this life is in him. He himself is this eternal life. He gives us this life by giving us Himself. Will you simply take Him today to be all that you need? It is not Jesus *plus* something else. It is simply Jesus Christ as all that we need, just Jesus!

CHAPTER 8

THE REAL JESUS OR ANOTHER JESUS

"For if he that cometh preaches another Jesus, whom we have not preached, or if ye receive another Spirit, which ye have not received; or another gospel, which ye have not accepted, ye might well bear with him"

2 Corinthians 11:4

Paul is declaring that there is another Jesus, instead of the real One and another spirit, instead of the Holy One, and another gospel instead of the true gospel. John said that the two main results of the true everlasting gospel is to fear God and give Him the glory (Revelation 14:7, 8). Therefore, if a gospel does not include giving God all the glory and the fear of God; then it is not the everlasting, true gospel.

If someone receives what they *think* to be the Holy Spirit, but *this* spirit causes them to *not* focus on the Lord Jesus,then this is probably *another* spirit. How can we know if it is another Jesus? The answer is found in Hebrews 13:8 *"Jesus Christ the same yesterday, and today, and forever"*

Jesus has never changed and He never will change. He is forever the same in character, in power, in purity and in the manifestation of his person. The Pharisees were trying to act like God, to be like him and this was the leaven. They wanted others to think this was the real true God, but it was a cheap imitation. There is no comparison between men in their flesh, soul, or human goodness and the true real Jesus Christ. There is absolutely no comparison and no similarity. Jesus is all-together different, and he is of another realm altogether. A major key to use is what Paul called, "the mind of Christ" Paul said to the church in Philippi; to let this mind be in you that was also in Christ Jesus 2000 years ago.

If the body of Christ wants the real Jesus to live inside of them; then they must receive his mind. The word Paul used for mind actually refers to an attitude of heart. If the body of Christ chooses the mind that was in Christ's physical body 2000 years ago; then the same Jesus will be able to live in his spiritual body on earth today. The main aspect of this mind of Christ is his servant hood, his humility, his obedience and his making himself of no reputation in the eyes of others (Philippians 2:5-8). Jesus had no desire to be seen in a good way by others; he only desired to be pleasing to his Father.

My reputation is how others see me, but my character is how God sees me. Jesus made himself of no reputation; therefore when a group chooses to let Jesus' mind be in them, they will not be wondering what others are thinking about them. There is a big difference between trying to be like Jesus and letting the mind of Christ be in you. If I am trying to be like Jesus, then this becomes an imitation of the real and this is another Jesus. If I am receiving the mind of Christ, then the real Jesus will live his very life inside of me. The real Jesus will always first take possession of a person's heart, and then his character will shine through them. The other Jesus will look like Jesus on the outside, but on the inside will be all kinds of uncleanness, pride, jealousies, etc. This is why Jesus had to tell the Pharisees, *"...ye are they which justify yourselves before men; but God knows your hearts, for that which is highly esteemed among men is an abomination to God"* (Luke 16:15).

The real Jesus will say exactly what is on his heart, and he will mean exactly what he says. This other Jesus will say something with his lips, but he will have some hidden meaning behind what he says. Sometimes, it will be *very difficult* to know exactly what he is saying. This person will not say exactly what he means and mean exactly what he says.There will be hidden agendas behind the words that this other Jesus is speaking.

The people that listened to Jesus said that no man ever spake like this man. His words were so real, so pure, so clean and so loving! There was no mixture in anything that he ever said. You could always trust him that whatever came out of this mouth was totally true and genuine. This other Jesus will say yes to you; but deep down inside of his heart, he wants to say no to you. The real Jesus will say what he means, and he will mean what he says. He will never try to say something to make you feel good, but he also will never try to intentionally hurt your feelings. He will always say exactly what you need to hear and it will always be with love and compassion.

The real Jesus is always filled with pure love; therefore he never needs to *act* like he loves you. Love is constantly coming out of him (through his words, through his thoughts, and through his actions). The real Jesus does not have to react to adverse situations because He is always in control. So, even if the people are about to throw him over a cliff, he will just walk right through them without any fear (Luke 4:28-30). This other Jesus appears very similar to the real Jesus, but when adverse situations come, he will react with fear or anger. The real Jesus has only one agenda: He desires to do the will of his father (John 17:4). This other Jesus has many hidden desires which are buried in his heart. The real Jesus will do miracles because he loves people and he desires to let them know that their heavenly Father's heart is full of compassion towards them. This other Jesus performs miracles only to be seen of men. Many times, the real Jesus would heal people then say, "tell no one." The real Jesus always put the greatest emphasis on the heart of his disciples (Luke 6:17-49).

Brothers and sisters, is the real Jesus living in your body, or is it another Jesus? The main characteristic of the real Jesus is his pure love. He is not selfish, He is kind (I Corinthians 13:5). The other Jesus can react with much hardness and irritation. The real Jesus is patient, even when people are taking a long time. The other Jesus is very impatient. The real Jesus is never envious of another person. He has no desire to have things, the other Jesus can be very jealous if someone has something and he doesn't have it. The other Jesus feels rejected when others are not noticing him. The real Jesus never needs to be noticed by others. The real Jesus is not provoked by silly and foolish behavior of others. This other Jesus is always trying to correct others and put them right. The real Jesus thinks thoughts that are true, honest, just, pure, lovely, and worthy of praise (Philippians 4:8). The other Jesus will allow his mind to think evil of others (1 Corinthians 13:4-5). The other Jesus is always trying to impress people and he will convince himself that the reason he does this is to help them. The true reason that he is always trying to impress people is because deep down inside, he wants them to like him. The real Jesus never needs others to like him, because if he did, this would prevent him from doing God's will. If a person needs to be liked by others, then they will not say some things that others will not like them to say. This other Jesus cannot speak the truth because of his need to have others like him. The real Jesus will always speak the truth and he will always speak it in love.

Am I Living like a Squirrel?

The Christian life is from another realm. It is the very real life of God. Therefore, if someone is trying to live the Christian life it can be compared to a squirrel trying to be a human. Vegetable species cannot become animal species and animal species cannot become human species and human species cannot become a divine species. This new created life is a divine species. It is the very life of God (divine nature) being lived inside of our bodies. *"Know ye not that your body is the temple of the Holy Ghost?"* (1 Corinthians 6:19). Jesus wants to come back into his church and live his very own life in his body on earth. *"Behold, I stand at the door and knock; if any man hear my voice, and open the door, I will come into him and sup with him and he with me"* (Revelation 3:20).

This is Jesus talking to his body; the church at Laodicea. Can it be possible that Jesus' body has kicked him out and now He is having to knock in order to be allowed his rightful place back into his church?

Am I a Self-Made Man or a God-Made Man?

Esau was a worldly man that the world would admire. This man is a man which depends on his own ability and doesn't see his need for the blessing of God on his life. It is time to fight for the great privilege of being a king and a priest. It is time to get our birthright back through Jesus Christ. Jesus came to restore man to his calling and purpose as a king and priest. Like Jacob, we must desire and fight for our birthright. God said that he loved Jacob and hated Esau. Jacob had a deep desire to have and to know the ways of the Spirit. Esau had a great desire to enjoy the ways of this world. God hated Esau, but loved his brother Jacob.

Why did God have such a special love for Jacob? Jacob saw his need for the blessing of God on his life. Jacob was someone who sought God's blessings because he realized that without God, he could do nothing. Jacob wanted the birthright from his brother. He deeply appreciated the very thing that his godless brother despised. Jacob needed all the blessing and favor of God that was offered to him. Esau lived as though he could do everything in his own strength. He had no need for God. An amazing thing about Esau was that he did things outwardly that would appear godly, but inwardly his heart was very ungodly.

Esau named his eldest son Eliphaz, meaning, God is his strength. He named his second son Ruel, meaning, "Friend of God". His third he named Jeush, meaning "to whom God hastens". His fourth was Jaalam, meaning "whom God hides". His fifth son he named Magdiel meaning, "The praise of God". Esau had such a wicked heart in the sight of God and yet named his children such Godly names. God will never accept what is done on the outside if it does not come from the sincerity of one's heart.

Human goodness will do so many things with the outward appearance of good. It gives others the impression that it loves God, but on the inside, its heart can be filled with no desire for the things of God! On the other hand, Jacob might have appeared to have an ungodly heart. However, God saw deep inside of Jacob's heart that he really desired to know God. Even though he did things like deceiving his father, his heart was pleasing to the

Lord. Esau with the names he chose for his children appeared to really care about the things of God, but it is absolutely clear that he cared nothing for the things of God. At one point, Jacob wrestled all night until he received blessing from God. His heart really desired God and it showed through his perseverance.

Hundreds of years ago a minister of the gospel called Richard Baxter wrote the following:

> *"The principal part of selfishness consists in an inordinate self-love. This is a corruption so deep in the heart of man, that it may be called his very natural inclination, which therefore lies at the bottom, below all his actual sins whatsoever; and must be changed into a new nature, which principally consists in the love of God. This is original sin itself, even the heart of it. This speaks what man by nature is; even an inordinate self-lover; and as he is, so he will act. In this, all other vice in the world is virtually contained. Every man is an idolater, so far as he is selfish."*
>
> Practical Works of Richard Baxter, London, 1883, S. 394-95

Am I Ishmael or Isaac?

Ishmael was the product of man's ingenuity but Isaac was the result of God's promise. My dear brothers, are we men who have been made by the ingenuity of self? Have we trusted in our own abilities and learning? If we had to give a one word answer to the question, "Who gets the credit for my life?" would our answer be God or ourselves? The Word of God says *"Blessed is the man that trusts in the Lord, and whose hope the Lord is"* (Jeremiah 17:7). The Word also declares that the Lord planned a masterpiece for our life and this plan was purposed for us in Christ Jesus before we were physically born. *"For we are his workmanship, created in Christ Jesus unto good works, which God hath before ordained that we should walk in them"* (Ephesians 2:10). The word for workmanship actually means a masterpiece. On the other hand, the Word of God says, *"Cursed is the man who trusts in man, and maketh flesh his arm and whose heart departs from the Lord"* (Jeremiah 17:5). God says that if a man trust in his own heart, he is a fool (Proverbs 28:26). Jesus said that all mankind is to deny themself (Luke 9:23).

Am I a self-made man or am I a God-made man? God has an eternal plan for my life prepared for me to walk in and thereby become a masterpiece, a handiwork of God himself. If we walk in His plan for us; trusting in His Spirit to make us what we ought to be; then our life will reveal to the world what God can create. He is called our Maker because He made us. Jesus said, "I will make you fishers of men" (Matthew 4:19).

So many men have forsaken the plan of God for their lives, and instead they invented their own plan and trusted in their own intellect to guide their steps. Can you imagine an inventor creating a toy and then the toy decides to do its own thing! Father God is our Maker (Isaiah 45:9, 11; 54:5) and He has an eternal plan for our life and we are to trust our life in his hands and choose to obey his will. This choice to trust and obey God allows him to form us according to His plan.

Since the Lord is a Master Artist, He will create the loveliest masterpiece and people will be in awe of His ability to create. The only requirement that the Creator has is that the clay vessel is given to the potter to do with it what He desires (Jeremiah 18).God does not need my ability. He is not hindered by my inability. He only requires my availability. The main reason for troublesome, perilous times in the last days is men who go to church and claim to be believers in a supernatural being called God will be lovers of their own selves!

> *"This know also, that in the last days perilous times shall come. For men shall be lovers of their own selves, covetous, boasters, proud, blasphemers, disobedient to parents, unthankful, unholy, Without natural affection, trucebreakers, false accusers, incontinent, fierce, despisers of those that are good, Traitors, heady, highminded, lovers of pleasures more than lovers of God; Having a form of godliness, but denying the power thereof: from such turn away"*
>
> 2 Timothy 3:1-5

Verse two says that perilous times will come at the end because men will be lovers of their own selves. In verse five we read that these same men will hold to a form of godliness, but deny the power of godliness. These men will love themself and go to a church gathering, but deny the power to be godly. This word for godliness means a true love for God, deep devotion and reverence for God.

The inner truth in the heart of these individuals is that they have an external appearance of loving God (like attending church services), but inwardly they love and trust in their own selves. This is the main reason for all the trouble that is coming on the earth in the last days. Lovers of self instead of lovers of God! Self-made men that attend church everywhere, but they will not trust God to make them, change them and live through them.

We Are Not Able

The entire Israelite army said we are not able to defeat Goliath (1 Samuel 17:24). They all saw what they could not do. The 10 spies for the Promised Land said, *"We be not able to go up against the people; for they are stronger than us"* (Numbers 13:31).

They all saw what they were not able to do. Joshua and Caleb saw what the Lord could do and so they said, *"If the Lord delight in us, then he will bring us into this land"* (Numbers 14:8). David saw only what the Lord could do and this is why he told Goliath, *"Today, the Lord will give you into my hand, so that the whole earth will know that there is a God in Israel"* (1 Samuel 17:46). Jesus said that the flesh profits nothing, but the Spirit gives life (John 6:63).

The pride and self-centeredness of man's heart can be so deceitful that a father can live his entire life as a selfish, self-made man and congratulate himself on a job well done. Maybe it appears from the outside that he did well. He worked hard, he made a good living (plenty of financial income), he provided a warm house for his family. He paid for his children to go to college and everything appeared to be very blessed. This man's pride could easily convince him that he was a successful person as a husband and a father. This describes an Esau type of man. Everything looks right on the outside, but what exactly is the truth on the inside and in the invisible realm of the Spirit? Maybe this man is blessed in one area; his finances. Although in many other areas he is cursed. His mind is full of confusion; his emotions are disturbed, unpeaceful and he gets angry easy and his family is fearful when they are in his presence. This self-made man is blinded by the pride of his heart. Like Esau, the pride of his heart deceives him (Obadiah 1:3).

When someone lives only by what he can see on the outside; he will only discover what his natural mind understands and perceives. Lot saw the land and it looked like the Garden of Eden on the outside, but in truth, this land was full of murder, hate, lust, and all kinds of evil. The land was called Sodom and it defiled and destroyed almost all of its inhabitants. If a man lives in the natural realm, depending only on what he knows, thinks, feels and believes; then a favorable wind will come his way and he will assume it is time to set sail for his desired haven.

> *"Now when much time was spent, and when sailing was now dangerous, because the fast was now already past, Paul admonished them, And said unto them, Sirs, I perceive that this voyage will be hurt and much damage, not only of the lading and ship, but also of our lives. Nevertheless the centurion believed the master and the owner of the ship, more than those things which were spoken by Paul. And because the haven was not commodious to winter in, the more part advised to depart thence also, if by any means they might attain to Phenice, and there to winter; which is an haven of Crete, and lieth toward the south west and north west. And when the south wind blew softly, supposing that they had obtained their purpose, loosing thence, they sailed close by Crete. But not long after there arose against it a tempestuous wind, called Euroclydon. And when the ship was caught, and could not bear up into the wind, we let her drive. And running under a certain island which is called Clauda, we had much work to come by the boat: Which when they had taken up, they used helps, undergirding the ship; and , fearing lest they should fall into the quicksands, strake sail, and so were driven. And we being exceedingly tossed with a tempest, the next day they lightened the ship; And the third day we cast out with our own hands the tackling of the ship. And when neither sun nor stars in many days appeared, and no small tempest lay on us, all hope that we should be saved was then taken away. But after long abstinence Paul stood forth in the midst of them, and said, Sirs, ye should have hearkened unto me, and not have loosed from*

> *Crete, and to have gained this harm and loss. And now I exhort you to be of good cheer: for there shall be no loss of any man's life among you, but of the ship. For there stood by me this night the angel of God, whose I am, and whom I serve, Saying, Fear not, Paul; thou must be brought before Caesar: and, lo, God hath given thee all them that sail with thee. Wherefore, sirs, be of good cheer: for I believe God, that it shall be even as it was told me."*
>
> Acts 27:9-25

We read in verse 13, *"When a south wind blew softly, supposing they had obtained their purpose"* These were self-made men who governed their lives by what they perceived, what they had learned in life and what they felt and thought they should do. Paul was a God-made man. First, he had to be knocked off his high horse by a blinding light of glory (Acts 9:3-4). Afterwards he had to learn of the Lord and to listen to the voice of God. Therefore, Paul knew that what the angel told him would come to pass no matter what it appeared to be on the outside.

Jesus said that if we are going to enter into the reality of true life; a life that is from heaven; then we must lose our natural life. All dependence on our self and all that we can accomplish apart from God's immediate intervention must be abandoned (John 12:25).

Esau believed he was a success; he had plenty of money, plenty of servants and lots of everything on the outside. But, the truth according to God is that Esau was an abomination (Proverbs 16:5). God hated him (Malachi 1:3), he walked in total deception, and his family was cursed. One of his grandchildren called Amalek was so hated by God, that God said I will wipe out the memory of Amalek off the face of the earth (Exodus 17:14-16).

There are many men who attend church every week and they believe that they are a success, but they have failed to see the truth about the mental, spiritual, emotional and eternal well-being of their families. Their children hate God in their hearts; their family walks in the same pride and deception as these men and in the invisible world, the powers of darkness have great power over these families.

Pharisees and Sadducees were good examples of these types of individuals. On the outside, they appeared to be true lovers of God. Jesus said your worship of me is in vain (useless) (Matthew 15:7-9). They thought that they were esteemed children of God. The truth was that they were children of the devil and their whole ancestral line was a breed of snakes. The venom of Satan's poison (pride) was still very real and operative in their blood line (Matthew 12:34).

A Plant that must be Rooted Out

Jesus said over and over that only what God does will last and only what has its roots in Him will bear eternal fruit. By their fruit, you will know them (Matthew 7:20). There is a big difference in being religious on the outside and the reality of the living Christ on the inside. Many times in the Scriptures, the Holy Spirit reveals to the reader the inner truth of someone's heart. This is because whatever we do secretly will be revealed by the Father openly (Matthew 6:3, 4; 6-8, 16-18, Luke 16:10-15). This can be very good if your name is Joseph, David, or Daniel; it can be very bad if your name is Pharisee or Sadducee! Many times I have witnessed families being destroyed in the spiritual, invisible realm, but the head of that family (father or husband), was in total deception; not even knowing that his inner man was bringing so much evil into his family. He was the main reason that his family was uncovered in the spirit, because he did not cover them.

The Lord says that a self-made man is cursed, a fool and heading down a wrong path. There is a way that "seems" right to a man, but in the end it is discovered that this way was simply the way of death (Proverbs 14:12). When a person starts to go away from God and God's ways, he leaves the narrow way that leads to life and is now walking on the broad way to destruction (Proverbs 14:14, Matthew 7:13). A self-made man will often be so deceived that he will not even perceive that he is to blame for the calamities that his family experiences. Therefore, he will blame God (in his heart), and he will blame others. He will actually think that he did things right and he "cannot understand" why things turned out the way they did.

Dear brothers, let us now pray like David did unto the Lord. Dear Lord, search us and know our hearts and see if there is any wicked way in us (Psalm 139, 23, 24). Once the Lord has uncovered any evil way in us, then he can lead us in the everlasting way. The everlasting way is the ancient path that leads right into the heart of Father God. This is the way of the eternal Lamb: someone who is totally dependent on his father to do everything through him; for without him, he can do nothing (John 5:19, 30).

It has always been the Father's plan to fully express his deity through our humanity. A God-made man is a true man; one in whom God's life accomplishes all things. A God-made man is totally dependent on God for wisdom, righteousness, love, holiness, peace, humility and everything necessary for life and godliness (2 Peter 1:4). The lie of the devil that mankind has swallowed is: we can be men apart from the very indwelling life of God. The spirit is the outcome of God breathing his very life into men's nostrils (Genesis 2:7). James said that the body without the spirit is dead (James 2:26). Therefore, God is life and we can only experience true manhood by receiving God as life in our human vessel of clay.

Man's Knowledge Instead of God's Life

The evil one said to Adam and Eve, *"You don't need God; you shall be as god."* Mankind believed the liar and he became an individual self that no longer required the need for the only True Self. One can only find his true self through union with God; who is the actual only True Self. It is from Him that mankind receives their life. God is life and without Him, we can do nothing. Man became a false self, posing as the true self. But, in the day that he ate from the tree of knowledge, he lost God's life and he became the source of his own life. Men took the place of God and they became a false self. This is the self that Jesus Christ says must be denied (John 12:25, Luke 9:23, Matthew 16:24, Mark 8:34). Once the devil got inside of Peter and Jesus looked straight at Peter and said, "Get behind me Satan" (Matthew 16:23) then Jesus said, *"You are a stumbling block to me Satan because you always set your mind on the things of men and you do not understand the ways of God"* (Matthew 16:23b).

The real problem is not the devil, the real problem is the believer in Christ that does not deny himself. When we refuse to deny self, this then opens an invisible door for the evil one to come into our mind. Right after Jesus rebuked the devil in Peter he said, *"If any man will come after me, let him deny himself"* (Matthew 16:24). We are God's field and God's garden and every plant that the Father has not planted will be plucked out. One day the disciples told Jesus that the Pharisees and Sadducees were offended at what he said to them. Jesus said to his disciples, *"every plant, which my heavenly Father hath not planted, shall be rooted out"* (Matthew 15:13). *"Let them alone, they be blind leaders of the blind. And if the blind lead the blind, both will fall into the ditch"* (Matthew 15:14).

A self-made man has been deceived into thinking that he can of his own ability, knowledge and strength accomplish God's will. A God made man realizes that without God's deity indwelling man's humanity, there is no true life and therefore no true humanity! Peter thought that he would not deny the Lord. Peter was trusting in himself to live for God and stand up for his Master. Peter totally failed as he denied his Master three different times.

One day God found a man that could be indwelt by Him to accomplish His divine purpose on earth. This man was called Moses, but Moses saw his own capability to accomplish what only God was able to accomplish. God had to deal with Moses for 40 years until Moses saw that he had no more ability to accomplish God's purpose on earth. Then, the Lord said to Moses, *"I AM come down"* (Exodus 3:8). God was trying to take the burden off Moses and encourage him with the fact that He was going to do the work *through* Moses, but Moses had to get his focus off of himself and on to God. Moses had to see that God did not need Moses' ability and He (God) was not hindered by Moses' inability! God does not need my ability and he is not disturbed by my total inability. Hallelujah! All that God requires is my availability! Hallelujah! Another person that was frustrated with God and fearful of the enemy was Gideon.

> *"And the angel of the Lord appeared to him, and said unto him. The Lord is with thee, thou mighty man of valour. And Gideon said unto him, oh my Lord, if the Lord be with us, why then is all this befallen us? And where be all his miracles, which our fathers told us of, saying, did not the Lord bring us up from Egypt? But now the Lord hath forsaken us, and delivered us into the hands of the Midianites. And the Lord looked on him and said, Go in*

> *this thy strength, and thou shalt save Israel from the hand of the Midianites" Have not I sent thee? And he said to him, oh, my Lord wherewith shall I save Israel? Behold, my family is poor in Manasseh, and I am the least in my father's house. And the Lord said to him, surely I will be with thee, and thou shalt smite the Midianties as one man"*
>
> Judges 6:12-16

If we are self-made; then we can be either depressed by what we cannot do or impressed by what we can do. Gideon saw all that he could never do and the Lord spoke this living word to Gideon. "Thou mighty man of valour, the Lord is with thee". Then the Lord said "Go now in this thy strength". Gideon's strength was to be discovered in the mighty, all-powerful living Word that was sent to him. However, after Gideon had won many battles and saw all that God could accomplish through Him; then Gideon built a statue to himself toward the end of his life (Judges 8:27).

A God made man trusts in the Lord, and sees what the Lord God can do for him, in him and through him and his gaze is fixed on the Lord. A self-made man will trust in himself, even his devotion to God, instead of denying himself, he exalts himself or pities himself; depending on whether he is pleased or rejected with himself.

My dear beloved brothers, may we as men humble ourselves for not revealing to our families and to our world true manhood. From this very day may we start to embrace our sentence of death, so that we may not anymore trust in ourselves, but in the God who raises the dead (2 Corinthians 1:9). He will live His very own life in us through His risen, exalted Self. He will forgive us, cleanse us and make us, because He is the Lord, our Maker! Gideon and King Saul were two examples of men that never really could get their focus off of themselves. On the other hand, Moses and Peter were excellent examples of men that did get their focus off of themselves and onto God!

CHAPTER 9

THE ETERNAL PURPOSE: A CORPORATE CHRIST

Christ is the Christian life. He himself risen and exalted is the life of a Christian. The Christian life is a Person. Therefore, if the Christian life is a Person; than how about the church. Most definitely; the church is also a Person. Here are some scriptures that declare this tremendous fact:

"And hath put all things under his feet, and gave him to be the head over all things to the church, which is his body, the fullness of him that fills all in all" *(Ephesians 1:22, 23)*. Paul is saying that the church is the fullness of him that fills all in all.

> *"For we are members of his body, of his flesh, and of his bones. For this cause shall a man leave his father and mother, and shall be joined to his wife, and they two shall be one flesh. This is a great mystery: but I speak concerning Christ and his church"*
>
> Ephesians 5:30-32

> *"And have put on the new man, which is renewed in knowledge after the image of him that created him; where there is neither Greek nor Jew, circumcision nor uncircumcision, Barbarian, Scythian, bond or free; but Christ is all, and in all"*
>
> Colossians 3:10-11

Paul is declaring a fact; that the church is a new creation, created in God's Son and Christ himself is all and in all. The risen and exalted Son of God is the very essence of the church. The church has its beginning at the resurrection of Christ. *"For as the body is one, and hath many members, and all the members of that one body, being many are one body; so also is Christ"* (1 Corinthians 12:12). Here Paul is referring to the body of Christ as being Christ.

> *"And Saul, yet breathing out threatening's and slaughter against the disciples of the Lord, went unto the high priest" "And he fell to the earth, and heard a voice saying unto him, Saul, Saul, why persecutes thou me?" "And he said, "Who art thou, Lord? And the Lord said, 'I am Jesus whom thou persecutest'"*
>
> Acts 9:1, 4, 5

This scripture is very clear. Jesus told Saul that he was persecuting him. In other words, the disciples of the Lord and the Lord are the same. Christ is the substance and the essence of the Church. Church is a not a building that someone goes to with other believers. Church is the ascended Lord clothing himself, with a people to reveal who He is to the world. Apart from the resurrected Christ living inside of people, there is no church.

One of the most fascinating revelations is to discover that almost every single reference in the New Testament to answered prayer, the baptism of the Holy Spirit, the eternal plan and the heart-beat of the Father is in the plural tense and not the singular. This signifies that the plan of God is related to a body and not just an individual. For example, the Father's promise to baptize with the Holy Spirit and fire is for a body. We tend to look upon this promise as something that "I" need. But, the tremendous truth is that it is something that Father wants to bestow on a body; something that "we" need and not something that *"I" need. "For John truly baptized with water; but you all shall be baptized with the Holy Ghost not many days hence"* (Acts 1:5). *"But you all shall receive power, after that the Holy Ghost is come upon you all; and you all shall be witnesses unto me both in Jerusalem, and in all Judea, and in Samaria, and unto the uttermost part of the earth"* (Acts 1:8). *"And, behold, I send the promise of my Father upon you all; but tarry you all in the city of Jerusalem unto you all are endued with power from on high"* (Luke 24:49). All of these references to the Baptism of the Holy Ghost are in the plural. In other words, the Father has always wanted to totally immerse an entire company of people with the Holy Spirit, power and fire from on high. I do not know if the church has really even seen the significance of this deep desire in the heart of the Father to fill a body with the very Sprit of his exalted Son (John 7:37-39). Maybe, one of the main reasons that the real power of God has not been seen in the church by the world is that the church has not seen the all-importance of the entire body. On the day of Pentecost they were all baptized as one body and then, *"they had all things common and no man claimed that anything that he had was his own"* (Acts 2:44-47). As a result of the early believers being filled with the Holy Spirit, they were of one heart and one soul and no one claimed that anything was his own (Acts 4:32).

"And with great power the body gave witness that Christ was indeed risen" (Acts 4:33).

The secret to having great power and grace is to live in fulfillment of Jesus' prayer that the church be one (John 17:11, 20, 21, 22, 23). This is a prayer that everyone claiming the name of Christ would lose their own individual, independent selves and would be one body. When the church becomes one, then Christ is all. As long as we Christians are letting the devil divide us, separate us and exclude us, the earth sees a totally divided and fragmented Christ. For the body to be one, each member must deny their self and all of their self-centered motives and agendas.

Now is a spiritual season with an abundance of grace to live for God and his divine purpose. We were saved so that we could be a part of a new man; one that would be the very image of his Maker and would do the will of the Father. Jesus delighted to do the will of God. *"I delight to do thy will, O my God; yea, thy law is within my heart"* (Psalm 40:8).

When someone embraces the cross; their old self-centered self is crucified in Christ and a new God centered and others centered self is birthed in them. The following Bible verses reveal Paul's revelation about how a New Covenant believer is to live his new life.

> *"Or do you not know that your body is a temple of the Holy Spirit who is in you, whom you have from God, and that you are not your own? For you have been bought with a price"*
>
> 1 Corinthians 6:19, 20

> *"And He died for all, that they who live should no longer live for themselves, but for Him, who died and rose again on their behalf"*
>
> 2 Corinthians 5:15

> *"For not one of us lives for himself, and not one dies for himself; for if we live, we live for the Lord, or I f we die, we die for the Lord; therefore whether we live or die, we are the Lord's"*
>
> Romans 14:7-8

All of these verses show that since we died in the body of Christ crucified, now we are to live in his resurrected self. This will only be accomplished through Him and by taking our place in Him. This is the glorious revelation of Romans chapter 6.

> *"What shall we say then? Shall we continue in sin, that grace may abound? God forbid. How shall we, that are dead to sin, live any longer therein? Know ye not, that so many of us as were baptized into Jesus Christ were baptized into his death? Therefore we are buried with him by baptism into death: that like as Christ was raised up from the dead by the glory of the Father, even so we also should walk in newness of life. For if we have been planted together in the likeness of his death, we shall be also in the likeness of his resurrection: Knowing this, that our old man is crucified with him, that the body of sin might be destroyed, that henceforth we should not serve sin. Now if we be dead with Christ, we believe that we shall also live with him:"*
>
> Romans 6:1-8

Since we have died in His body and we have been raised with him, now we are to live in continuously believing and reckon ourselves dead to sin and alive to God in and through the exalted Christ (Romans 6:11).

The Father's Heart to unveil his Son in the Body

Paul said, it pleased the Father to reveal his Son in him (Galatians 1:16). And, if Father is pleased to reveal his wonderful Son in Paul, surely he is pleased, to reveal his Son in the entire body of Christ. We read in Galatians 4:19 "My little children, of whom I travail in birth again until Christ be formed in you all." This is the plural form and therefore Paul's burden of travail had to do with the resurrected Christ being formed within the entire body at Galatia. After Christ revealed himself as the very reality and substance of the church; which is his body to Saul (Acts 9:1-6), he seemed to have a major passion to see Christ come to fullness in his body in Galatia. Travail, agony and pain to see Christ formed in the church at Galatia (Galatians 4:19).

EPHESIANS

Paul had a deep desire that the body would not be discouraged by his suffering which was for their glory (Ephesians 3:13). He desired Christ to dwell in the inner man by the Spirit within the entire body of Ephesus (Ephesians 3:16-21). Paul desired the Ephesus believers to walk worthy of this great calling; which was to have Christ formed in them (Ephesus 4:1-10). He yearned for the entire body to come to fullness. He stated that this fullness was the stature of the very measure of all that the risen exalted Christ is today (Ephesians 4:13).

COLOSSAE

Paul's burden once again was to unveil the mystery; which is Christ in you all as a body (Colossians 1:27). Again, this is in the plural and therefore it is referring to the entire body at Colossae. Paul even rejoiced in his suffering for the entire body at Colossae (Colossians 1:24) so that this mystery of Christ can be fulfilled in his body. Paul yearned that every single member would be presented complete or perfect in Christ. He even declared that it was the very energy and power of Christ in him that was working mightily trying to bring the body to fullness (Colossians 1:28, 29).

THESSALONICA

> *"And the very God of peace sanctify you (all) wholly; and I pray God your whole spirit and soul and body be preserved blameless unto the coming of our Lord Jesus Christ. Faithful is he that calleth you (all), who also will do it"*
>
> 1 Thessalonians 5:23, 24

Once again, Paul is writing to the entire body of Christ at Thessalonica with a passion to see Christ set them apart entirely to the Father. Apparently, after Paul saw the risen Christ as the very church that he was persecuting; the eyes of his heart were opened to see how the Father looks at the church! I regret that for so many years I did not have the revelation of how precious the body of Christ really is. Until it has been revealed that Christ is in every believer; a person cannot really understand that what they do to one of the least of these, they do to Christ. Paul had to share with the fleshly carnal believers of Corinth that he wanted to give them so much more truth, but they could not receive it yet (1 Corinthians 3:1-5). Their selfishness was blocking them from receiving the revelation of Christ in his body. Paul tried to share with the Corinthian body that every member is very important and the whole body is full of Christ (1 Corinthians 12:12-27). You all are the body of Christ and members in particular (vs. 27). We are one and we need each other in order that the full revelation of Christ can now come to the world through the church; which is his body (Ephesians 1:22, 23).

Answers to Prayer

Many times Jesus uses the plural in reference to a believer receiving answers to prayer.

> *"And whatsoever ye (all) shall ask in my name, that will I do, that the Father may be glorified in the Son. If ye (all) shall ask anything in my name, I will do it. If ye (all) love, keep my commandments. And I will pray the Father, and he shall give you (all) another Comforter, that he may abide with you (all) forever; even the Spirit of truth, whom the world cannot receive, because it seeth him not, neither knoweth him; but ye (all) know him; for he dwells with you (all) and shall be in you (all). I will not leave you (all) comfortless, I will come to you (all). Yet a little while, and the world seeth me no more, but ye (all) see me. Because I live, ye (all) shall live also. At that day ye shall know that I am in my Father, and ye (all) are in me and I in you (all)"*
>
> John 14:13-20

> *"Abide in me, and I in you (all). As the branch cannot bear fruit of itself, except it abide in the vine; no more can ye (all) except ye (all) abide in me. I am the vine, ye (all) are the branches; He that abideth in me, and I in him, the same bringeth forth much fruit; for without me ye(all) can do nothing. If a man abide not in me, he is cast forth as a branch, and it is withered, and men gather them and cast them into the fire, and they are burned. If ye (all) abide in me, and my words abide in you (all), ye (all) shall ask what ye (all) will, and it shall be done unto you (all). Herein is my Father glorified that ye (all) bear much fruit;*

> *so shall ye (all) be my disciples. As the Father hath loved me, so I have loved you (all), continue ye (all) in my love. If ye (all) keep my commandments, ye (all) shall abide in my love; even as I have kept my Father's commandments and I abide in his love. These things have I spoken to you (all) and that your joy might be full"*
>
> John 15:4-11

All of these verses are talking to a group of disciples.

> *"And in that day, ye (all) shall ask me nothing, verily, verily I say unto you (all) whatsoever ye (all) shall ask the Father in my name, he will give it to you (all). Hitherto, have ye (all) asked nothing in my name; ask, and ye (all) shall receive, that your joy may be full. At that day ye (all) shall ask in my name; and I say not unto you (all) that I will pray the Father for you (all), For the Father himself loves you (all) because ye (all) have loved me, and have believed that I come out from God"*
>
> John 16:23, 24, 26, 27

There are many more Scriptures about God yearning to hear the body pray as one man; but we will just refer to one more portion of Scripture.

> *"Therefore, I say unto you (all) what things soever ye (all) desire, when ye (all) pray, believe that ye (all) receive them, and ye (all) shall have them. And when ye (all) stand praying, forgive, if ye (all) have aught against any; that your Father also which is in heaven may forgive your trespasses"*
>
> Mark 11:24-25

Beloved, these last two verses are talking to the body of Christ. Christ is saying that if a body will pray in faith, and since faith works only by love (Galatians 5:6) then it is necessary to have nothing in your heart against anyone. To have aught is to be holding onto something that someone did to you in the past. To forgive is to throw out what you have been holding onto. Throw it out once and for all. So, Father God is wanting a body of believers to pray in faith, with nothing in their hearts towards anyone and then they shall receive whatever they are asking for!

Some Christians say, "I can love the world, but I struggle with loving Christians" I used to say this as a Pastor and as a Christian that really loved Jesus. I now realize that the only reason that I could love the world, but struggle with other Christians is because I judged the Christian and I did not judge the world. We cannot have love and compassion for anyone that we are judging. Jesus said he did not come to judge the world, but to save it. We must see the body of Christ as a realm or a habitation, where the ascended Lord dwells. Christ is all within his church; which is his body.

The King's Eternal Law

"If ye fulfill the royal law according to the scripture, Thou shall love thy neighbor as thyself, ye do well" (James 2:8). This royal law is our King's law since the beginning of time. Jesus talked often about this law. It is called, the Law of Mercy, the Law of Love, the Law of Christ or the King's Law (the Royal Law). Jesus said, *"Whatsoever ye would that men should do to you, do ye even to them; for this is the law and the prophets"* (Matthew 7:12). The King's law from the very beginning of creation has been that I shall love my neighbor as my very self or I shall do to others what I want them to do to me.

One time, I heard the Lord say you shall not love your neighbor as your neighbor, but you shall love him as your very self. Then, He continued to explain this to me, if I love my neighbor as my neighbor; then I will look at him and I will start to see all the differences between him and I. The basic root meaning of the word to judge is to make a distinction. This is what Jesus was saying in reference to himself in John 5:30. *"I can of mine own self do nothing; as I hear, I judge; and my judgment is just; because I seek not mine own will, but the will of the Father, who sent me."* Jesus said as I hear, I judge. In other words when a thought or voice came to the man Jesus, he had to make a distinction as to where that thought or voice came from. If it came from himself, then he could not receive it because he only came to do the Father's will. If it came from the evil one; then he definitely had to reject it.

When I love my neighbor as my neighbor, I will make all kinds of judgment on him because of his color, culture, style, and many other things. But, if I love my neighbor as my very self, then I will do to him (in thought, word or deed) what I want him to do to me. When a person gets saved and receives the risen and ascended Lord into them; now they should have the fire of God's love burning in them for all people; but especially for other believers. We are commanded by our Lord to love one another with the same kind of love that he has (John 13:34, 35). This is the only way that the world will know that we are the disciples of Jesus, because they will see the pure love of Jesus in us. There will be more miracles, more answers to prayer, more evangelism and more fruit than ever if only we could let the risen, exalted Christ come back in and take over his church. And maybe the best of all, the Father's heart will be greatly satisfied when He sees his Son filling his body!

Dear family in Christ, the Lord is calling forth a remnant who will become a flame of pure love for him. Our God is a consuming fire (Hebrews 12:29). In the center of this flame is the purest, most holy love imaginable. The *actual interpretation* and meaning of Song of Songs 8:6 is *"set me as a seal upon your heart, as a seal upon your arm; for love is as strong as death the jealousy of love is as unyielding as the grave."* This jealous love must possess the one it loves, without letting it go. Its flames emanate from Jehovah; a most vehement flame. This passionate consuming love is so strong that nothing can quench it.

> *"Many waters cannot quench love, neither can the floods drown it: if a man would give all the wealth of his house instead of love, it would be utterly despised" (Song of Songs 8:7). John said, "How can I love God, whom I cannot see, when I don't love my brother; whom I do see?"*
>
> 1 John 4:20

This is the hour to see the ascended Christ as the very life and essence of his entire body. Whatever we think about our brothers and sisters, we are thinking about Christ. Whatever we do to our brothers and sisters; we are doing to Christ himself. Whatever we say about our brothers and sisters; we are saying about Christ. Now, is the time to manifest the body of Christ and not just teach it. This revelation of the corporate Christ will transform our concept of church and Christianity. Father God wants us to take responsibility for one another and not be like Cain who said, "Am I my brother's keeper?" Who put that thought into Cain's heart? 1 John 3:12a "Not as Cain, who was of that wicked one" (1 John 3:12a). Cain was of that wicked, evil one and he, the devil put that thought into Cain's heart. The evil one was a murderer from the beginning (John 8:44).

Within the context of the new humanity called the church; we are one family with one Father. This is why Jesus said, *"John, behold your mother"* and to Mary he said, *"Woman, behold thy son"* (John 19:26, 27). There must be a body today that is filled with all the fullness of the Son and they will be consumed with the same heart of love and compassion. Compassion is a key to allowing God's pure love to flow through a body.

> *"But whosoever has this world's goods, and sees his brother in need, and shuts up his heart of compassion from him, how does the love of God abide in him? My little children, let us not love in word or in tongue, but in deed and truth"*
>
> 1 John 3:17, 18

When someone closes their heart of compassion, then God's pure love stops flowing and human love takes over. God's pure love requires compassion as an invisible channel to flow through. Jesus was moved with compassion for people. Compassion simply means to suffer with another. Compassion is when a person allows their heart to feel the pain and hurt that others have experienced. When I close my heart of compassion, I am making a decision not to feel the pain of the other person. The Lord is full of compassion (Psalm 145:8). When a vessel is full; then there is no more room for anything else. Within the kingdom of God, people are treated like a brother and sister. Six times in the epistles; we are told to greet one another with a holy kiss. Jesus referred to his grown men as children. Paul referred to the body as little children and John likewise. Children is a family term and a kingdom word and when God is our father, then this is the way His children talk to each other. Also, greeting one another with a holy kiss is the way God's family greets each other.

We read Ephesians 4:6 that the Father is above all, through all and in all within the body of Christ. People will look so different when we look at them through the Father's eyes! In the following statement I must be real honest and include myself. We have failed. We have so failed as a body that is called to be indwelt and filled with the resurrected Lord. We have failed to love one another. Paul and John both said there is nothing that is as important as God's love dwelling in us. If we don't have the love of God living in side of us, then God says our life counts for nothing.

Miracles, gifts, sacrificial service all amount to nothing if they are not coming out of a heart that is full of the love of God (1 Corinthians 13:1-3). Jesus commands us to love our enemies, but we haven't been able to even love our brothers and sisters yet. Christian families are constantly struggling and why is this so? The number one reason that Christian families and marriages are failing is a lack of the pure love of Jesus. With all the soulish attempts to be like Jesus, we have failed so greatly in the area of just letting Jesus himself live in and through us. Jesus took the blame for the entire world. Why is it so hard for us to take the blame if it will bring peace, harmony, unity and love and keep the peace in God's family? Many of our ancestors have failed to walk in the love of God and we should identify with their sins as an act of corporate repentance. We see very precious godly servants of the Lord like Daniel, Nehemiah, Ezra, Paul, Moses doing this. It is time for the body to start to repent as a body. "If my people, which are called by ma name, shall humble themselves, and pray, and seek my face, and turn from their wicked ways, then I will hear from heaven, and will forgive their sin, and heal their land" (2 Chronicles 7:14). The first ancestor that we should identify with is Adam, because it is his selfish nature that we have inherited. We should take the blame and ask for mercy and deny our self. Then we should identify with the holy, lowly nature of Christ as we renounce self, we should allow Jesus to come into our midst with all of his fullness. We cannot keep identifying with the sinful desires, thought patterns and judgments of our ancestors once we come to Jesus. We must decide; do we want to continue to walk in selfishness or do we want to walk in love? We must confess, ask forgiveness and allow the cross to destroy the power of hate that is within our bloodline. The blood of Jesus has the power to destroy the evil that is in my old bloodline. Jesus has conquered for me on the cross and now He wants to conquer in me by his Sprit.

The greater the revelation of the body of Christ is, the more we will understand when one member suffers, we all suffer (1 Corinthians 12:26). The more that we see the corporate Christ that is taking up residence in his body; the greater will be our faith in him to restore, to keep, to transform the members in his body. *"Who art thou that judgeth another's man servant; to his own master he stands or fall. Yea, he shall be holden up; for God is able to make him stand"* (Romans 14:4).

The indwelling Lord is able to make the weak and the faltering brother to stand. So many times we try to do God's work for him. This becomes a way of interfering and not a way of helping. We can now trust much more in all that Christ can do in our brothers and sisters. He is able to make them stand. He is their keeper. This is not saying that a person doesn't bring correction, but it must be at the right time and there should always be prayer first so that their heart will be receptive. So much correction is done in the soul and it comes out of pride; thinking that I am able to change the situation. He is always able to change a situation.

CHAPTER 10

A NEW COVENANT AND AN OLD WAY

For thousands of years the Lord has been calling people back to the ways of the Lord. Over and over again, the prophets have been calling the people to walk in the ways of the Lord. These ways do not change, because He is the same yesterday, today and forever (Hebrews 13:8).

The goal of the New Covenant is to bring people back to the original plan of God, which is to have a people in His own image, after his likeness. This heavenly people will now become his people and He will be their God and Father. This is a new covenant that is intended to bring people back to an old way of life.

From the very beginning, man could choose between the tree of life or the tree of knowledge which would then bring death into them (Genesis 2:9, 17; 3:22). Since the fall, mankind has been feeding on his fleshly, worldly knowledge. This has produced the fruit of pride, self-exaltation and criticism; these are all things which the Lord hates (Proverbs 3:5, 6; 1 Corinthians 8: 1, 2; Ephesians 4:17, 18; 2: 1-3). Jesus told the Pharisees that their worship of God came from what they learned intellectually, and not out of their heart (Isaiah 29: 13, Mark 7:7-23; Matthew 15:9). True worship can only come from one's heart once they have received a revelation of who God is. When the Lord reveals himself to a person, then they will have a true godly fear of the Lord.

If someone only receives teaching, then their fear of God will not be a true godly fear (Isaiah 29: 13). God said you have been taught to fear and love me and therefore you choose to do it, but it does not proceed out of your heart. Eating from the forbidden tree brought into us the nature of the rebel which is pride and rebellion against God. Men turned away from their Creator and his ways, and rebellious hearts became stubborn and hard. Men did not fear God from their hearts and so they walked in their own ways. The true fear of God will always give someone a desire to please the Lord and to walk in his ways. Many times the Lord spoke to his people that if they would walk in his ways; then they would be blessed. Curses, troubles and judgments come to a person that refuses to walk in the way of God. God the Father sent John the Baptist to prepare the way of the Lord and to make his paths straight (Luke 1:76; 3:4, 5; Isaiah 40: 3-7). John's message as the voice of One in the wilderness was a loud declaration that men must repent and turn from their selfish, sinful ways. We read in Isaiah chapter 40, the full message of this prophetic end-time voice and it is the utter frailty of flesh and human ability, and the complete separateness of God! God told Jeremiah to tell his people to get back to the ancient, old ways (Jeremiah 6: 14-16; 18:14-16). Jesus Christ is the Way and within his very Person is contained all of the ways of God. (Matthew 11:28-29; John 14: 6; 1 John 1:1-4). God desired men to eat from the tree of life and this would have resulted in eternal life constantly flowing into them and through them (Genesis 3:22). This tree of life always brings healing to all people of all nations (Revelation 22:1, 2; John 7:37, 39).

In the beginning, God gives His own life for His creation in the form of the tree of life (Genesis 2:9). Men were never supposed to be the source of their life. Then, God made a blood covenant with Abram and a blazing torch and a flaming oven passed through the pieces of the dead covenant animals (Genesis 15:17, 18). The Lord put Abram to sleep while He; the Pre-incarnate Christ walked through the pieces instead of Abram (Hebrews 4:3, 9, 10; Revelation 1:13-15). God revealed to Moses that the Word was in them and the Lord was their very life (Deuteronomy 30: 11-14, 20). Paul through a tremendous revelation of the Word (Colossians 1:25-27), understood that the law was to be lived through an indwelling Lord and not through a natural ability (Romans 10: 4-13). The problem with the old Covenant was with the people. The covenant only failed because the people failed (Hebrews 8:8, 9). The people tried to live the law out of their own ability, instead of out of the indwelling presence of God. Not only did the Lord give His Holy Spirit to live in them, but He himself writes His law on the inside of a believer's heart.

Father has accomplished everything for man through the earthly body of His Son. The Spirit of Christ wants to bring to fullness in the spiritual body of Christ what He has accomplished in the physical body of Christ (Hebrews 9:14, Ephesians 3: 16-21, 4:13). From the very beginning, men have broken their covenants with God, because they trusted in themselves instead of the Lord (Hosea 6:7, 10:12, 13 and Jeremiah 17:5, 7).

God has put all life in the body of his Son and whoever has the Son has the life (1 John 5:11, 12). Whoever does not have the Son, does not have this eternal life. God the Father has made an eternal covenant with His Son and only those who are in Christ can partake of the benefits of this covenant. Every person comes into the world in Adam. When they join themselves to the Lord, the Father places them into Christ (Ephesians 1:3; 1 Corinthians 6:17; Colossians 2:9, 10). Now, the Father, through His Spirit wants to accomplish in each member of Christ what He has already accomplished through the physical body of His Son (Hebrews 10:10, 14). All of the ways of God are contained in the person of Christ (John 14:6; Psalm 40:7, 8).

Men choose their own way instead of God's way (Isaiah 53:6; Proverbs 14:12; Proverbs 2:25-33). Through Jesus, one will now fear the Lord and greatly delight in all of His commandments (Hebrews 13:20, 21; Philippians 2:13). Now, the original plan of God can be fulfilled through a people called Christians or the body of Christ. God can bless these people because now they fear the Lord, delight in His commandments and love on another. This is all quite possible because Jesus is risen and living in them. David said, *"Blessed is every one that feareth the Lord; that walks in his ways"* (Psalm 128: 1). In Psalm 112, we are given wonderful blessings for fearing the Lord and delighting in His ways.

The Lord's intention has eternally been to have a people for His own possession, but this could only be fulfilled as they lived their lives as vessels for Him to possess. Instead of allowing God to possess His people, they became vessels for a self-centered spirit (Ephesians 2:1-3; 1 John 5.19). The Father, Son and Holy Ghost made an eternal agreement or covenant with each other before the foundation of the world. The Son agreed to die and deal with this sin nature in flesh (Romans 8: 3). He would completely fulfill all the requirements of the holy law of love in which mankind has totally failed. His blood would pay the penalty for man's transgressions. The debt will be totally and fully paid (John 19:30). Through this all men can be forgiven of every violation of the Father's divine, holy and just laws (Luke 24:47). The Son agreed to this out of his love for the Father (Psalm 40: 8). In response the Father agrees to completely pardon all mankind if they come to the mercy seat. He could command the enemy to release the captives. He made the Son's name the highest and most exalted, glorious name through all the universe. Most of all, the Father gave the Son a very special promise, a gift for His body on earth. No longer would the Spirit be restricted to a few individuals, but now He allowed him to pour the Spirit out on all cleansed flesh (Luke 24: 49; Acts 1:4, 5, 8; 2:1-3, 32, 33).

Lastly, the Spirit of God is saying, "I will glorify the Son in every possible way. I will magnify His office, reveal His character, and exalt His triumph. I will convict the world of their relationship to the Son and I will give many supernatural gifts to the body on earth. I will reveal to everyone that will listen, all that the Father has given to you!

The Most Essential Promise for these Days

The key to the Father's heart being satisfied is the precious promise of the Father to His Son. It is only through this gift, that the body of Christ on earth; which is the church can fulfill their purpose. The fullness of the presence and power of the Holy Spirit is the promise that the Father made to His Son. Any local body of believers can receive this baptism of the Holy Spirit and fire in faith and consecration.

The Father delights to pour out His Spirit to whatever measure that there is a real desire for Him (Luke 11:13). Every local assembly of believers should expect and wait for a full baptism from on high (Luke 24:49). This can only be received by faith. In Acts 19:2, Paul asked some Christians if they have received the Holy Ghost since they have believed. Faith is the main requirement for this precious gift from the Father (Galatians 3:5, 14). There must be an expectancy regarding the gift of the Spirit. If there is expectancy, then the praying will be more and more intense.

The faith of the body will increase and now the asking will become seeking and the seeking will become knocking (Matthew 7:7, 8).

Father God desires to reveal the fullness of His Son to the world. Fullness will only manifest once the body is filled and saturated with the Spirit of the Son. God's will can only be done through God's Spirit in God's way. The flesh profits nothing. Jesus prayed that His body on earth would be one, just as the Father and He are one. Only as the Holy Spirit fills the body with Himself, will the body lose their self (Luke 9: 23). Now; the result will be a full revelation of a risen glorious Lord Jesus in His body on earth. *"And let him that is athirst come. And whosoever will, let him take the water of life freely"* (Revelation 22:17b).

CHAPTER 11

A MINISTRY OF THE SPIRIT OR A MINISTRY OF THE SOUL

Am I ministering life to others within the body or am I ministering death? Many times if someone is only releasing knowledge and doctrine; this can produce more pride in the hearers. *"Knowledge puffs up, but love builds up"* (1 Corinthians 8:1). Knowledge about the word of God can actually make a person feel more spiritual because they possess spiritual truth. But this is not life, this is only doctrine. People that receive more and more teaching without the impartation of life will grow fat and lazy.

Jesus said that there was one parable that was essential for his followers to understand. This parable was the parable of the sower and the seed (Matthew 13:17-23, Mark 4:1-20). The soil is the heart and the seed is the Word of God. There are four kinds of soil and three of them have things that block the seed from growing; things like hardness, thorns (cares of this world) not enough moisture (no brokenness), the evil one coming immediately to steal the seed of God, etc.

One type of soil is the good soil. Jesus said that tribulation comes because of the Word. This means that when the word comes to us in revelation, it comes with a shell around the outside. Like in the natural realm, God uses tribulation to break the shell and then the life in the center of the seed comes forth in the midst of the tribulation.

This is why both James and Peter tell the body to rejoice with every type of trial and tribulation (1 Peter 1:5-7, James 1:2). When a believer stands in the midst of trials and gives thanks, this opens the way for the real life of Christ to manifest through the believer. The real life is in the seed and not in the knowledge or the feeling. Tribulation must come in order that the inner life of Christ can come through the broken shell. It is only through brokenness, that one can have the release of life in their ministry.

Knowledge and teaching only feeds the mind, but life can change the very inside of a person. *"And if Christ be in you, the body is dead because of sin; but the Spirit is life because of righteousness"* (Romans 8:10). What comes out of our body or soul is death; but what comes through the Holy Spirit through our human spirit is life. Jesus said, *"It is the spirit that quickeneth; the flesh profits nothing; the words that I speak unto you, they are spirit, and they are life"* (John 6:63). The flesh and the soul profits nothing, but the Spirit through our spirit gives life. Paul said that he served God in his spirit (Romans 7:6, Colossians 1:8, Romans 8:16; Romans 1:9).

A ministry of the spirit comes through many dealings with our natural self or soul. If a speaker is bound up with what is in his mind, and what he is feeling; then he will release what is in his soul, instead of what is on the mind of the Spirit within his spirit. If the Holy Spirit wants to cry through the speaker; but he is unbroken in the area of his feelings, then he cannot be a vessel for the Holy Spirit to use until there is more brokenness. A person can be so full of himself in the form of doctrine, feelings, and thoughts, that he cannot release what is burning on the heart of God. The flesh profits nothing, but the spirit gives life. My words are spirit and life.

One time Peter allowed the devil to speak through him and he said to the Lord, *"Be it far from thee Lord; this shall never be unto Thee"* (Matthew 16:22b). Jesus turned to Peter and said, *"Get thee behind me Satan: thou art an offence to me; for thou savourest not the things that be of God, but those that be of men"* (Matthew 16:23). When we set our mind on the things of men; the Holy Spirit is prevented from revealing to us the things of God. One day the disciples came to Jesus and said that there are Greeks that wanted to see him (John 12:20-26) His response was shocking. He basically said the world is going to see my risen Self after there has been a death and there was no other way. Death will always precede resurrection and it is through the resurrection that Christ is revealed within his body. A seed must go into the ground and die and then it will bear much fruit. He is referring to the fruit after its own kind; which is the life of Jesus Christ. The body must die to themselves in order that Jesus can come through them.

This process of death will come in many different ways, but in each one there will be a struggle to get off the cross and come down. There must be a firm stand at the cross; whereby I accept my sentence of death and God must now raise me and release a spiritual ministry through my life. *"But we had the sentence of death in ourselves; so that we should not trust in ourselves, but in God who raises the dead"* (2 Corinthians 1:9).

> *"But we have this treasure* (Christ) *in earthen vessels* (us), *that the excellency of the power may be of God, and not of ourselves. We* (in our soul and body) *are troubled*

> *on every side, yet not distressed* (Christ in us)*; we are perplexed, but not in despair* (Christ in us)*; persecuted* (on the outside), *but not forsaken (*full of strength on the inside), *cast down, but not destroyed. Always carrying about in the body the dying of the Lord Jesus* (the power of the cross to slay the selfish nature in us), *so that the life also of Jesus might be made manifest in our body,* (this is the real Jesus himself, His risen Self). *"For we which live* (in this world) *are always delivered to death for Jesus sake, so that the life also of Jesus might be made manifest in our mortal flesh. So, then death works in us; but life in you* (all)*"*
>
> 2 Corinthians 4:7-12 (words in parentheses are the authors)

Paul is declaring a tremendous truth that it is only as Christians stay on the cross and allow the death of Christ to constantly work in them, and then the very risen life of Christ will flow through them. Every believer should come together allowing the cross to work in them. Paul is trying to communicate this in Romans 12:1. *"I beseech you (all) therefore, brethren, by the mercies of God, that ye (all) present your bodies a living sacrifice."*

Every time there is a gathering of the saints (the children of God); they should come together as one sacrifice that is alive only to God. Then, the world would see a visible demonstration of that acceptable, good, and perfect will of the Father on earth (Romans 12:2). However, if we gather together and there is a secret desire to get something for self, then we will not be able to release life to the other believers.

In Philippians 1:15-17 we are told about two kinds of preachers. Both are preaching Christ with their lips, but on the inside one is preaching Christ with a "contentious spirit". A good synonym for contentious would be selfish ambition. The word actually means to be seeking something for one's self. While preaching Christ, I can still want the people to vote for me. On the other hand, the other preachers are preaching Christ with pure love in their hearts and God's love never seeks anything for self (1 Corinthians 13:5).

The men who are preaching Christ out of love are releasing what Paul refers to as the *"supply of the Spirit of Jesus Christ"* (Philippians 1:19). Do I minister life to others or am I just seeking to get from others? If we learn to stand in the midst of slander, lies and opposition; then the Holy Spirit will create a ministry whereby He can release the very life of Jesus through our spirits.

CHAPTER 12

THE RESURRECTED CHRIST OR SELF

Who do I want the whole earth to behold when they are beholding me? Christ wants to clothe himself in my humanity so that He can show the world what He can do through an earthen vessel. This was the secret to David's life. Goliath, the Philistine caused the entire army of God to tremble. They were all terrified at the face of one man. The entire army looked at Goliath and then they looked at themselves and they concluded that there was no hope. *"And all the men of Israel, when they saw the man, fled from him, and were sore afraid. And the men of Israel said, have ye seen this man that is come up?"* (1 Samuel 17:24, 25a). They could never defeat a warrior like Goliath. David was just a boy that knew his God, looked at the situation in a totally different way. David saw Goliath, but David remembered how he depended on the Lord to deliver him from the lion and the bear.

> *"Thy servant slew both the lion and the bear; and this uncircumcised Philistine shall be as one of them, seeing he has defied the armies of the living God. David said,*

> *moreover, the Lord that delivered me out of the paw of the lion, and out of the paw of the bear, he will deliver me out of the hand of this Philistine"*
>
> 1 Samuel 17:36, 37

David had one great desire that burned in his heart and he told Goliath this is the main reason that he would destroy him.

> *"This day will the Lord deliver thee into mine hand; and I will smite thee, and take thine head from thee; and take thine head from thee; and I will give the carcasses of the host of the Philistines this day to the fowls of the air, and to the wild beast of the earth; so that all the earth may know that there is a God in Israel"*
>
> 1 Samuel 17:36-37

David's passion was to let the whole earth know that God lives in his people. David wanted to demonstrate to the army how God fights their battles and gives them the victory. He wanted the whole entire earth to see how great his God was in him. He did not desire to show the world how great things he could do, but how great his God was inside of him.

John the Baptist said, *"He must increase, I must decrease"* (John 3:30). The Lord is yearning to reveal his greatest glory through his sons on earth (Romans 8:19). He must increase in his body and the personalities of flesh must decrease!

The Holy Spirit is the Spirit of Truth and he will only relate to his children on the basis of truth. Every man's way is right in his own eyes (Proverbs 16:2), and therefore every man will say "I want Jesus to be seen in me", but, the Lord will test our hearts to see if this is the truth. *"Howbeit in the business of the ambassadors of the princes of Babylon, who sent unto him to inquire of the wonder that was done in the land God left him, to try him, that he might know all that was in his heart"* (2 Chronicles 32:31). *"The Lord is nigh unto all that call upon him to all that call upon him in truth"* (Psalm 145:18).

We will all be tested and we will prove if we really desire the Risen Christ to be exalted in us or if the truth might be that deep down inside we want others to acknowledge us. What we do on the outside is what people are seeing, but who we are on the inside is what God sees. This is the reason why it is so important to God how I treat my wife, my children and family. It is easy to be insensitive to the needs and feelings of those closest to you. If a person chooses to be sensitive and kind instead of hard and indifferent, then this choice reveals much to Father God.

How do I react when I am honored and spoken well of? How do I react when I am dishonored and ignored and spoken evil of? It is a necessity to first clearly understand the tremendous difference between the religious self-righteous self in all of us, and the real resurrected Christ. Underneath what appears to be love, concern and kindness can be anger, self-pity, selfish motives, jealousy, pride and rage!

With the risen Christ there is nothing hidden, it is all pure love and holiness. It is the brightest, most glorious attitude of love and compassion. There is total truth without an ounce of any deceit. Because of the deception of the human heart, deep down inside, a person can actually believe that they are not much different than Jesus. The truth is that Jesus is the life of the believer and Jesus is the life of his church, but there are so many hidden areas of self that is blocking the real Jesus from manifesting himself in his church. Where is our hope and what is our trust for the future? *"It is better to trust in the Lord than to put confidence in man. It is better to trust in the Lord than to put confidence in princes"* (Psalm 118: 8, 9). This is the exact center of the entire Bible. These two verses are in the very middle of the entire Bible. This is one of the most vital truths in the entire Bible. It is better to trust in the Lord, than men or princes. Jeremiah said it in a much stronger way.

> *"Thus saith the Lord, cursed be the man that trusteth in man, and makes flesh his arm, and whose heart departs from the Lord. For he shall be like the heath in the desert, and shall not see when good comes, but shall inhabit the parched places in the wilderness, in a salt land and not inhabited. Blessed is the man that trusts in the Lord, and whose hope the Lord is. For he shall be as a tree planted by the waters, and that spreads out her roots by the river, and shall not see when heat comes, but her leaf shall be green; and shall not be careful in the year of drought, neither shall cease from yielding fruit"*
>
> Jeremiah 17:8

Are we looking, expecting our united efforts to change society? Do we trust in the many good things of humanitarianism to change people's lives? Are we trusting in another method or another program? Or maybe we are hoping next year things will get better? Where is our trust? What are we hoping in to change our situation, society or our nation? Are we trusting in the real, tangible living presence of the God who said, *"I will never leave you or forsake you"* (Hebrews 13:5). Are we trusting in what men can do, or are we truly trusting in what God can do?

God does not want even consecrated self; a self that has been consecrated to the Lord, so that the Lord can use this servant in his vineyard. No, the Lord wants a crucified self and not a consecrated self. The Lord is looking for an empty vessel that

He will live his very life through. Self is no good, even if it is consecrated; it will still depend on its own ability and it will be the source of its power. But, the Lord has clearly decreed not by might or by power, but by my Spirit, says the Lord of Hosts (Zechariah 4:6). We will not truly expect the Holy Spirit to do everything in us and through us until we see the vital truth that I can do nothing out of myself (John 5:19, 30; 15:5). The one that sees that he can do nothing out of himself; now can start to expect his humanity to be the house for the living God to dwell in. The Father needed a body to reveal his personality through for the world to behold (Psalm 40, Hebrews 10, John 1:18). Even so, Jesus Christ needs his body to reveal his radiant, glorious self through for the world to behold. Our bodies have been purchased by the priceless, precious blood of the Son of God (1 Peter 1:19, 1 Corinthians 6:19, 20). Our bodies are now a home or temple for the Holy Spirit to live inside of. He owns our bodies and we are no longer our own. We have another owner. When a person lovingly and willingly present their body for the ascended Christ to live in (Romans 12:1), that person must now start to conform totally to the image of God. God, the Holy Spirit will never conform to what the person is thinking, believing or feeling. The Holy Spirit will always come in to take total possession of the person's spirit, soul and body. Faithful is he who calls you to a total separation of spirit, soul and body and He will also do it (1 Thessalonians 5:23, 24).

The risen Christ will come into live in all of his beauty, humility, mercy and love and he does not change. We must be in total agreement with him regarding letting him express Himself through our mortal bodies. Amos said, *"How can two walk together unless they are agreed"* (Amos 3:3). Self will try to live like Jesus. It will go to church, do nice things to people, read the Bible and pray; especially pray for others. Self will do so many things that will look good and convince others that this is the nature of God in that one. Do I really want the real, living, pure and ascended Christ to live in my body or do I trust in my ability apart from his very life in me?

CHAPTER 13

THIS VICTORIOUS, HEAVENLY LIFE

In this chapter we want to discover the secrets of living in this life daily. The victorious, heavenly life is simply God's own uncreated life in man for the purpose of revealing God to man. When Jesus Christ died on the cross, he died as the last Adam (1 Corinthians 15:45); this means that he took all of the fallen creation with him to the cross. He destroyed the power of the evil that controlled mankind since the fall in the Garden of Eden. When he rose again, He rose as the head of a new humanity and he is called the firstborn of a new creation (1 Corinthians 15:42-49, Romans 8:29, Galatians 6:15, John 20:17). After the resurrection, Christ entered into another heavenly dimension; another realm for now he could walk through walls without any restriction (1 Corinthians 15:6, John 20:26). He became a life-giving Spirit. This allowed him to breathe his resurrection life into his disciples and now they were his brethren and he was the first born and Father was his Father and also their Father (1 Corinthians 15:45, Romans 8:29, 2 Corinthians 3:17, John 20: 17-23, Hebrews 2:11).

For three and a half years Jesus Christ walked **with** his twelve disciples, but now he was going to live **inside** of them (John 14:16-20). Then Jesus ascended up into heaven. At Pentecost, the risen and ascended Christ returns to earth in the Holy Spirit and He fills 120 people and then 3000 people. Now, there is an actual living Christ dwelling on earth again, but this time it is as a corporate expression within the bodies of real, physical people. Jesus has returned just as He told his disciples. It is the ascended Christ dwelling within the spirits of his corporate body on earth. This is the true life of the church today. It is not the type of church building or doctrinal beliefs or numbers of people. It is only the people in whom the risen God-Man or Son of God is living inside of that constitute the church today. How do we get this life?

One begins by joining himself to the Lord (1 Corinthians 6:17). He comes into agreement that what the Lord is he desires to be (Amos 3:3). He repents of his old creation way of living, which is selfishness and he denies himself and embraces the cross (Luke 9:23, Matthew 16:24-26, 2 Corinthians 5:14, 15). All of this takes place through the gift of faith from above.

This then opens the door for the Father to place him into his all-conquering Son. Now, this individual is in a new realm and part of a new humanity (1 Corinthians 1:30, 2 Corinthians 5:17, Romans 6:4-6). Now the life of the risen Christ is living in his spirit (1 Corinthians 6:17). This life is not something to be earned or achieved. This life is *Someone* to be wholeheartedly received and loved and not something to be earned.

Next, this all conquering, all sufficient Lord desires to have full possession of his new home, but there are many areas that are closed off to him. These are areas where there are fears, wounds and bondages. The Holy Spirit will work faithfully to obtain total possession of these hidden areas (1 Corinthians 6:19, 20,

Romans 12:1,2; 6:13, 17; Psalm 51:10; 2 Corinthians 6:16, 7:1, Psalm 139:23-24, Hebrews 10: 19-22).

This living Christ can be grieved (Ephesians 4:30) or resisted and quenched (1 Thessalonians 5:16-19). More and more the Holy Spirit will come to strengthen and empower the body so that Christ can be more fully formed within them. This should be prayed for and expected on a regular basis (Ephesians 3:16-20).

One of the main areas where the indwelling Christ will desire to work is in the area of the sacrifice of praise. This is the fruit that He creates in the lips of his body. He (the living Christ) is a Christ of praise. He is always thanking and praising the Father. Now, this believer will eat the fruit of his lips, which is great blessings from above. *"Peace, peace, to him who is far off (both Jew and Gentile) and to him who is near! Says the Lord; I create the fruit of his lips, and I will heal him (make his lips blossom anew with speech in thankful praise)"* (Isaiah 57:19 Amplified Bible). *"A man's (moral) self shall be filled with the fruit of his mouth; and with the consequence of his words he must be satisfied (whether good or evil)". "Death and life are in the power of the tongue, and they who indulge in it shall eat the fruit of it (for death or life)"* (Proverbs 18:20-21 Amplified Bible).

Every tree bears fruit after its own kind and therefore, the living Christ is a tree of life and continual thanksgiving, rejoicing, and praise keeps the fire of His presence burning in a believer. (1 Thessalonians 5:16-19). "*By Him therefore let us offer the sacrifice of praise to God continually, that is, the fruit of our lips, giving thanks to his name"* (Hebrews 13:5). We are to yield our tongues to him to praise and sacrifice to his Father the sacrifice of thanksgiving; which is continuously acknowledging the name of the Lord. The all-conquering, all sufficient Almighty One who is totally sufficient for every situation is to fill our thoughts and mouths. His name is I Am!

This sacrifice of praise is a continuous sweet smelling aroma in the nostrils of the Father. It is prophesied of the risen Christ that He will declare his Father's name unto his brethren, in the midst of the church. He will sing praise to His Father (Hebrews 2:12). How can he sing unless we give him our lips to sing through?

The main way that we live in this risen life of the ascended Christ and He lives his very life in us is by yielding all of our members to him as a living sacrifice. This living sacrifice He will live inside of and work through.

> *"Neither yield ye your members as instruments of unrighteousness unto sin; but yield yourselves unto God, as those that are alive from the dead, and your members as instruments of righteousness unto God"*
>
> Romans 6:13

> *"I speak after the manner of men, because of the infirmity of your flesh; for as ye have yielded your members servants to uncleanness and to iniquity unto iniquity; even so now yield your members servants to righteousness unto holiness"*
>
> Romans 6:19

> *"I beseech you, therefore brethren by the mercies of God, that ye present your bodies a living sacrifice, holy acceptable unto God, which is your reasonable service. And be not conformed to this world; but be ye transformed by the renewing of your mind, that ye may prove, what is that good, and acceptable, and perfect will of God"*
>
> Romans 12:1, 2

> *"What? Know ye not that your body is the temple of the Holy Spirit, which is in you, which ye have of God, and ye are not*

> *your own? For ye are bought with a price; therefore glorify God in your body, and in your spirit, which are God's"*
>
> 1 Corinthians 6:19, 20

The only way that this risen, ascended Lord Jesus can live in and through us is as we each present every one of our members to Him. I must give him my eyes that He can look through. I must give him my feet so that He can walk through them, I must give Him my lips so that He can speak through, I must give Him my mind and imagination so that He can reveal His thoughts to me. This is not a passive blanking out of the mind; but instead it is an active presentation of one's mind to the risen Christ. All of my earthly members must be yielded to Him so that He can now express His personality, bear His fruit; reveal his heart and do His works through my entire body. He lives within my spirit, and then by many constant choices of my will, I present my soul and body to him to manifest Himself.

As a person learns to walk in their spirit, they will become more aware of His indwelling and His presence will get stronger and stronger within them. He will not stay locked up in my spirit or there would be no visible expression of His life in the world. He needs to reveal his emotions through our souls, and He needs to reveal his actions through our bodies.

The enemy will always try to poison our spirit, so that our speech will defile others. This is a major hindrance to the Risen Lord living through us. When Jesus speaks, it will be words that are refined seven times. His words are totally pure, without any mixture or poison (defilement). *"The words of the Lord are pure words. As silver tried in a furnace of earth, purified seven times"* (Psalm 12:6). Remember, how the enemy used Peter to speak to the Lord (Matthew 16: 22, 23). Just like Jesus wants to express himself through His body on earth, even so the devil wants to express himself through anyone that will open their mind and heart to him. (Ephesians 4:27).

Our risen Lord is a Consuming Fire (Hebrews 12:29). He is light (John 1:1-4; 1 John 1:5) and He is love (1 John 4:8). He will never come through a person with an unloving, spirit. This is the evil one. He will never come with any deceit, for He is light. He will never come with harsh, critical words; these are always coming from another spirit. Once, Jesus 'disciples wanted to call fire down from heaven, and Jesus said to them, "you do not know from which spirit you are from." In other words, you are letting another spirit speak to your mind! Jesus is full of compassion and pure love and He is looking for a body that He can express this compassion and pure love through.

There is a tremendous need today to understand the importance of the Body of Christ. We cannot express Him apart from His body on earth. I will repeat; we cannot express Him apart from His body on earth. Only in very rare occasions perhaps, like if you are banished to the Island of Patmos, then maybe for a time you will have a divine calling to be alone. But, every other time, I need to see that Christ is a Corporate Man and He lives in a body. Can you imagine saying, "I do not want to love my right leg today, so I will only love the rest of my body today." Or, I think I must cut off my left finger, because I do not agree with the way it writes on paper.

In order to love Christ, we must love his entire body. We cannot separate ourselves from the body of Christ because they choose to gather in a building with a steeple, or because they choose to gather in a house. We cannot choose to separate ourselves from the body of Christ if we are a part of that very body. This is very serious and we need revelation to see Christ. Christ fills his entire body with His very life. *"A man who isolates himself seeks his own desire; he rages against all wise judgment. A fool has no delight in understanding, but in expressing his own heart"* (Proverbs 18:1, 2 NKJ).

When someone separates themselves from a part of Christ's precious body, they probably have a hidden motive and that is to reveal their own opinions and to express their own heart. The body of Christ is a spiritual reality. First and foremost, the body of Christ is filled with spiritual life on the inside. It is not something that you can organize on the outside. It is a dynamic, vibrant reality in the spirit realm. Do not judge a book by its cover or a Christian by where they meet on Sunday. If we want to express the full manifestation of the exalted Christ, then it is going to take the full expression of His body. We need one another.

Three main blocks that hinder Christ from living his very own life in and through his people.

1. PRIDE (especially spiritual pride.) Jesus has the same hatred for the pride in me that He had for the pride in the Pharisees of His time on earth. God hates pride. *"Every one that is proud in His heart is an abomination to God"* (Proverbs 16:5). *"God will destroy the house of the proud"* (Proverbs 15:23a). *"God resists the proud"* (James 4:6; 1 Peter 5:5). Pride will cause Christ to resist me. He will not live through me if He is resisting me. He must resist this horrible, wicked heart attitude of pride that is found in the evil one (Ezekiel 28:17, 1Timothy 3:6). Never will Jesus manifest Himself when someone is allowing their pride to control them! Never! One main area where our pride will manifest in us is in our judgments of others. (see author's other books) Pride will always esteem itself better than another. If someone is

doing something that appears to be wrong, then the one walking in pride will feel justified in pronouncing judgment. There is a righteous form of judgment, but this is actually discernment or discipline. However, unrighteous judgments will always come out of our pride. The main way that a person will know that they have made an unrighteous judgment is a hard feeling towards the person they judged. If we cannot feel the tender love and forgiveness of Jesus, but instead we are always feeling irritated at someone, then there are judgments towards that one. If I am choosing to love my mother or wife but still feel irritated with them; then maybe this is a judgment operating in my blood line towards women.

We have seen thousands of precious people with judgments humble themselves. There comes a deep sense of the manifest Presence of Christ when this happens. We have seen this in the church body, families, couples and individuals. Wherever there is a humbling of oneself; then there will be a drawing near of the divine Presence. He seems to have a special love for humility. Humility is the very essence of God´s very own heart (Matthew 11:28-30).

We have witnessed people's lives that were totally changed because they humbled themselves. Then the presence of Jesus filled their hearts and home. However, sometime later, if they make judgments, speak hard words, blame each other and do not take the blame themselves, then the presence withdraws from their midst. We must learn that the heart of Jesus is full of humility, and He wants us to learn of Him regarding his lowly heart. If I really want Jesus to express Himself through me; then I will humble myself whenever my pride starts to manifest through me in any way.

2. FEAR – "There is no fear in love" (1 John 4:18a). "Perfect love casts out fear" (1 John 4:18). God is perfect love and if we will yield our members to Him; then He will cast out the

fear that is paralyzing me. Many times, the risen Christ wants to express himself to someone that needs a kiss, hug, or a kind word; but the one that Jesus is wanting to use has fear speaking to them. If this person listens to fear, then Jesus will not be able to reveal Himself through that person. We must give Jesus our arms, our lips, our eyes, everything so that He can reveal himself through us.

Jesus always loves his enemies and so if someone speaks evil to me; Jesus wants to love them through me. If I am depending on myself to love them, I will feel anger, fear or rejection and I will not be able to love them. But, if I choose to love and open my heart and yield my earthly members to Jesus; then He will express himself through me. Brothers and sisters, Jesus is ready to live in us and through us. Are we ready to let him live through us? The very person that aggravates you is the very person that Jesus has tremendous love and mercy for. Jesus does not feel about others the way we feel about them!

Do I really want Jesus to live in me?

This is a very important question because if I say yes; then this would mean that I would have to say no to my fears. When Jesus wants to love someone and my fears are telling me not to; I will need to ignore my feelings and allow Jesus to love them through me. Perfect love casts out fear and Jesus is perfect love. *"Now God himself and our Father, and our Lord Jesus Christ, direct our way to you, and the Lord make you to increase and abound in love toward one another, and toward all men, even as we do towards you; to the end that he may establish your hearts unblameable in holiness before God, even our Father, at the coming of our Lord Jesus Christ with all his saints"* (1 Thessalonians 3:11-13). This truth is stating that God's love should be always growing and abounding in us in greater and greater capacities. This love is first towards the body of Christ; one another and then it is towards all men. Next, this truth is declaring, that as we are growing deeper and deeper in love; then our hearts are being established in holiness in the sight of the Father. Love is the main aspect of God's holiness. The Spirit of the risen Christ will constantly strive to create within us more and more pure love to each other. John said that if we love on another, then God dwells in us (1 John 4:12). If we are living in the love of God by an act of our will, then we will present our bodies to love. The moment that someone senses that their heart is getting cold; they should repent and ask God to forgive them for their judgments and fill them with his love and thank Him. Cold love is a curse for any Christian and never should I be complacent if I feel that my heart is cold. My God is a Consuming Fire.

3. UNBELIEF – Jesus dwells in your hearts by faith (Ephesians 3:17). Faith works by love (Galatians 5:6). When we make the right choices to love and to allow the risen Christ to live inside of us; then we must receive Him by faith and expect Him to express Himself through us. Faith should not be complicated. It is simply expecting God to do what He says. He loves to live inside of us and reveal Himself to a needy world. Unbelief will prevent Jesus from manifesting His life, love, and power through me. The call on every single Christian is to have His life in my body, through my members, expressing His glory and love to people all around me. If we believe on Him; then rivers of living water will flow out of us to the world around us. This is referring to the Spirit of the glorified Jesus (John 7: 37-39). So often unbelief will cause someone to look at the result of their actions, instead of looking to Jesus and trusting Him to change them. Without faith it is impossible to please Him (Hebrews 11:6). There is no possible way to please God if we do not have faith. It is impossible! Anything that is not of faith is sin (Romans 14:23).

There is a big need today for spiritual fathers and spiritual mothers. Are we willing to be a vessel for Jesus to pour parental love through us? Will we let the real living Christ love through us out to the multitudes of people that need to feel a mother's touch? Will we allow the real Jesus to touch one of the millions of people who are yearning for the loving affectionate touch of a father? Am I giving out what I received from my earthly parents? Do people feel that I just want to put them right or that I want to correct them? Do people think that I want to control or manipulate them or force them to do what I think they should do? Jesus came to reveal the Father and today when Jesus is living through a vessel, others will experience God the Father's love coming through them. One of the greatest characteristics of the Father's heart is His gentleness. This is what made David the great man that He was (Psalm 18:35). If I am a vessel for the living Christ, He will want to express the gentleness of God through me. He will definitely want to be kind, merciful, loving, towards people; especially when they don't deserve it. This ascended and living Christ is looking for a body to fill with His very life. He is searching for a body to allow Him to show Himself through them (2 Chronicles 16:9).

Today, we can present our bodies to Christ to come in and live through us. But remember He will be the exact same Christ today as He was thousands of years ago. He never changes! He will love His enemies. He will do good to those who despitefully use Him. He will bless others who curse Him. He is knocking at the door now asking if He can come in and love through you. Will you let Him? Do you want the world to behold the risen Christ through you? The choice is yours!

CHAPTER 14

CONCLUSION

This book has examined a heavenly, victorious life. This heavenly, victorious life is none other than Jesus Christ risen and exalted today and living by the Holy Spirit on earth within a people called His body. Many Christians are trying to live this life out of their own ability, goodness, and strength. This will never work. These Christians will experience many discouragements and much defeat in their lives. This person tries to perfect in the flesh what God began in His Spirit (Galatians 3). He who began the good work is also He who will finish the work (Philippians 1:6). Of Him, through Him, and to Him are all things now and forever. To Him be all the glory for his marvelous grace. Somehow, Christ has been removed from Christianity. To replace Him, there has come religious works, human effort, human goodness, and many outward things to try to earn God's approval. But, the truth is that it is only the Son of God that is well-pleasing to the Father. Everything that the Son does pleases the Father. Today is a day of restoration, whereby, the Holy Spirit is preparing the body for a fresh baptism of fire.

This baptism of fire will empower the body to be filled with the risen Christ and His pure love. This body will then be equipped with supernatural gifts so that they can overcome the powers of the kingdom of darkness. This body will glorify and exalt the Son and His glory will be seen within them. As it was stated at the beginning of this book, if my Christianity does not work in my home; then it will not work anywhere. But, this baptism of love, whereby a person is filled with the actual, tangible presence of the risen Christ, will work in the home and family! When a person humbles himself to receive His risen life to replace their selfish life, He will fill them and His presence will have a definite effect on those around them. This is an hour of preparation. The church body is being prepared to have no other rival. They will have only one Lord, one husband, one love, one Father and one King and one kingdom agenda. Their deep desire is to seek His kingdom first and His righteousness, and to proclaim the kingdom of the one they deeply love! His glory is about to be seen in His body on earth and the earth has been groaning for this for thousands of years (Romans 8).

Jesus Christ has so many aspects of His being that it is impossible to fully describe Him. He has so many titles to his person such as: Son of God, Prince of Peace, King of Kings, Lord of Lords, Bridegroom, Master, Lamb of God, Bright Morning Star, etc. The full radiance of His glory is something that the Father desires the world to behold. Paul said that as we are beholding His glory, we are all being changed into that same image, from glory to glory (2 Corinthians 3:18).

Brothers and sisters, it is our choice to put Christ back into the center of everything and let Him have the total supreme pre-eminence, or we can be a part of a system that is going their own way and doing what they feel is best. The Holy Spirit has declared that in the church, Christ is all, and in the world He is Lord and

Ruler over all nations. One day, this One that has all the glory and power and authority will give it all back to His Father, so that God, the Father may be all and in all (1 Corinthians 15: 27-28).

Beloved brother or sister, at this very moment, is Christ at the very center of your life? Is He the source of all that you do? Is His Spirit your only hope? How important is His grace and mercy to you? Do you realize that apart from Him and His grace, you can do nothing? Why not allow Him to take over everything concerning you: your life, your walk with God, your family, your future, everything! Say to Him, "I am your vessel Lord, come and live your very life in and through me now."

A Closing Prayer

Heavenly Father, Thank you for all that you have given me when you gave me Jesus, thank you for the abundant supply of every good and perfect thing that I have in Him. May your heart be satisfied with my life. From this moment, I give you my body, soul, and heart so I can be a vessel for your Son to live through. I want Jesus Christ to clothe my humanity with his divinity today and forever, Amen. Thank you Father God!

OTHER BOOKS BY GREG VIOLI

Depression and Introspection: Healing for the Diseased Mind:
This book explains root causes for depression
and how the disease of introspection affects millions
and how it blocks a person from living in the presence of God.

The Lamb's Heart
This book is a thorough revelation of the spiritual heart and the heart of God. It has much truth concerning brokenness in the Father's heart and how to allow the Father to heal your own brokenness. Tremendous revelation concerning how and why God always looks at the heart of his creatures.

The Secrets of a Fantastic Marriage
This book reveals how to experience a fantastic marriage because it explains in an in-depth way how to live in the heart of God and to allow Christ to be formed within individuals.

The King's Holy Beauty
This book discusses the beauty of holiness, a deep revelation of the inner character of the kings of the two spiritual kingdoms.

Whose Image and Which Mind
This book is a crucial revelation of the eternal purpose of God including the differences between heavenly wisdom and earthly wisdom, the heavenly image and the earthly demonic image and much more.

For more information about Greg Violi, his ministry, itinerary, and materials visit the following websites:

www.aplaceforhisglory.com

www.erweckt.de

To arrange speaking engagements please use the following email address:

greg.violi.ministries@gmail.com

Made in the USA
Lexington, KY
08 February 2017